HOMELESSNESS: IS SOCIETY LOOKING THE OTHER WAY?

HOMELESSNESS: IS SOCIETY LOOKING THE OTHER WAY?

ERNEST P. TODD
EDITOR

Novinka Books
New York

LIBRARY OF CONGRESS CATALOGING-IN-PUBLICATION DATA
Homelessness : is society looking the other way? / Ernest P. Todd, editor.
     p. cm.
Includes bibliographical references and index.
ISBN 1-59454-652-5
1. Homelessness--United States. I. Todd, Ernest P.
HV4505.H6512   2005
362.5'0973--dc22   2005022046

3 9082 11088 4890

Published by Nova Science Publisners, inc. ✦ *New York*

CONTENTS

Preface   **vii**

Chapter 1   Homelessness: Recent Statistics, Targeted Federal
                 Programs, and Recent Legislation   **1**
                 Maggie McCarty

Chapter 2   Strategies for Reducing Chronic Street
                 Homelessness   **31**
                 *Martha R. Burt, John Hedderson, Janine
                 Zweig, Mary Jo Orti, Laudan Aron-Turnham
                 and Sabrina M. Johnson*

Index   **133**

PREFACE

The rich continue to get richer - thank goodness. And in the 21st century the homeless do not exist. At least that is what the media leads us to believe. And if they should - they deserve what they get. Very nice - especially if it were true. This book sheds some light on a subject that society hates to hear about - homelessness.

In: Homelessness
Editor: Ernest Todd, pp. 1-29

ISBN: 1-59454-652-5
© 2006 Nova Science Publishers, Inc.

Chapter 1

HOMELESSNESS: RECENT STATISTICS, TARGETED FEDERAL PROGRAMS, AND RECENT LEGISLATION[*]

Maggie McCarty

SUMMARY

There is no single federal definition of homelessness. However, most federal programs for the homeless define a homeless individual as a person who lacks a fixed and night-time residence or whose primary residence is a supervised public or private shelter designed to provide temporary living accommodations, an institution accommodating persons intended to be institutionalized, or a public or private place not designed for, or ordinarily used as, a regular sleeping accommodation for human beings.

Existing data estimate the homeless population in the United States as ranging from 600,000 to 2.5 million. A congressionally mandated Homeless Management Information System (HMIS) to count the homeless is expected to produce annual data about the number of homeless individuals beginning in late 2005.

A number of federal programs, most authorized by the McKinney-Vento Homeless Assistance Act (P.L. 100-77), serve the homeless. The main federal programs for the homeless include the Education for Homeless

---

[*] Excerpted from CRS report RL30442 dated May 31, 2005.

Children and Youth (EHCY) program; the Emergency Food and Shelter Program (EFSP); the Health Care for the Homeless Program (HCH); the Projects for Assistance in Transition from Homelessness (PATH) program; the Consolidated Runaway and Homeless Youth Programs (the Basic Center Program and the Transitional Living Program); the Street Outreach Program (SOP); the Supportive Housing Program (SHP); the Shelter Plus Care (S+C) program; the Section 8 — Moderate Rehabilitation of Single-Room Occupancy Dwellings (SRO) program; the Emergency Shelter Grants (ESG) program; the Homeless Veterans Reintegration Program (HVRP); the Health Care for Homeless Veterans (HCHV) program; and a number of other federal programs for homeless veterans.

Looking toward the future, the Administration has adopted a goal of ending chronic homelessness within ten years, and several proposals designed to help reach that goal have been introduced in the 109th Congress.

INTRODUCTION

There is no single federal definition of what it means to be homeless. However, most federal programs for the homeless use the definition of a homeless individual provided by the McKinney-Vento Act (P.L. 100-77):

> an individual who lacks a fixed, regular, and adequate nighttime residence; and a person who has a nighttime residence that is (a) a supervised publicly or privately operated shelter designed to provide temporary living accommodations (including welfare hotels, congregate shelters, and transitional housing for the mentally ill); (b) an institution that provides a temporary residence for individuals intended to be institutionalized; or (c) a public or private place not designed for, nor ordinarily used as, a regular sleeping accommodation for human beings.[1]

Recent Data on the Homeless

Data on the number of homeless individuals and families are largely unavailable. The only consensus is that the number of homeless persons is probably between 600,000 and 2.5 million. The homeless are notoriously difficult to count because of their nomadic nature and because so many of the homeless are not in shelters, but are on the streets or are doubled-up with friends and family. The Department of Housing and Urban Development (HUD) has undertaken a congressional mandate to implement a system that will provide an unduplicated count of homeless individuals and families who access homeless services. The Homeless Management Information System (HMIS) is currently being implemented across the country. It is anticipated that the first data should be available in December 2005.[2] Since HMIS data are not yet available, the best homeless data currently come from sample studies.

There are two major studies of the homeless. Although both studies provide an assortment of data on the homeless, neither includes an estimate of the total homeless population. The most recent report, "Hunger and Homelessness Survey: A Status Report on Hunger and Homelessness in America's Cities,"[3] an annual report sponsored by the U.S. Conference of Mayors, was released in December 2004. In order to conduct the study, the Conference of Mayors appointed 27 mayors to serve on its Task Force on Hunger and Homelessness. The cities where those 27 mayors serve were surveyed for the study.[4] The data from each of those 27 cities were compiled by an individual or agency in the city's government, and were reviewed by a senior-level manager before being submitted. For the 2004 survey, the data were collected from the cities for the period of November 1, 2003 to October 31, 2004 during November and December 2004, and were supplemented with data on population, poverty, and unemployment available from the Bureau of the Census and the Bureau of Labor Statistics.

The earlier of the two studies was released in December 1999. "The 1996 National Survey of Homeless Assistance Providers and Clients (NSHAPC)"[5] was designed and funded by 12 federal agencies[6] with guidance provided by the Interagency Council on the Homeless, a working group of the White House Domestic Policy Council. The U.S. Bureau of the Census collected the data based on a statistical sample of 76 metropolitan and nonmetropolitan areas between October 1995 and November 1996. The Urban Institute analyzed the data.

Specific findings of these two studies are summarized below. It is important to remember that these two surveys were conducted at different times, look at different geographical areas, ask different questions and use different survey techniques; thus the results are not necessarily comparable.

The 2004 U.S. Conference of Mayors Study

The U.S. Conference of Mayors (USCM) study seeks to track the changes in demand for emergency shelter and emergency food assistance, as well as changes in the characteristics of the homeless population. According to the most recent study, in 2004, requests for emergency shelter increased in the survey cities by an average of 6%, with 70% of the cities registering an increase. Requests for shelter by homeless *families* increased by 7%, with 78% of the cities reporting an increase. On average, people remained homeless for eight months (up from five months in 2003) and just under half of the cities reported that the duration of homelessness in their communities had increased over the previous year. According to the study, lack of affordable housing led the list of causes of homelessness. In order of frequency, the other cited causes included mental illness and the lack of needed services, substance abuse and the lack of needed services, low-paying jobs, unemployment, domestic violence, poverty and prison release. Regarding the demographics of the homeless population, the surveyed cities reported that, on average, single men comprise 41% of the homeless population, families with children, 40%, single women, 14% and unaccompanied youth, 5%. By race, the homeless population was estimated to be, on average, 49% African-American, 35% white, 13% Hispanic, 2% Native American and 1% Asian. The cities also reported that, on average, 23% of homeless people were considered mentally ill; 30% abused substances; 17% were employed; and 10% were veterans. The study also looked at access to housing assistance for the homeless in the surveyed cities and found long waits. Applicants must wait an average of 20 months for public housing (down from 24 months in the 2003 survey) and 35 months for Section 8 Vouchers (up from 27 months in the 2003 survey). Over half of surveyed cities had stopped accepting applications for at least one assisted housing program due to the length of the waiting lists.

The NSHAPC

Although the NSHAPC has not been updated since 1996, it is largely considered to be the most comprehensive data set available on the extent of homelessness, the characteristics of the homeless population, and service programs designed to serve the homeless. The study found that homeless clients were predominantly male (68%) and nonwhite (53%); 23% of homeless clients were veterans. Large proportions had never married (48%) and 38% had not received a high school diploma. The NSHAPC also found that 34% of homeless people found in homeless assistance programs were members of homeless families (defined as a client with one or more children) and that homeless families had, on average, two children. Parents reported that almost half (45%) of these children ages three to five attended preschool and that 93% of school-age children (ages 6 to 17) attended school regularly. Forty-two percent of homeless clients reported that finding a job was their top need followed by a need for help in finding affordable housing (38%). Fifty-eight percent reported at least one problem with getting enough food to eat during the 30 days before being interviewed. Thirty-eight percent of homeless clients reported alcohol problems during the past month, 26% reported drug problems, and 39% reported mental health problems during that period. Over one-quarter (27%) of homeless clients had lived in foster care, a group home or other institutional setting for part of their childhood. Twenty-five percent reported childhood physical or sexual abuse.

The NSHAPC counted approximately 40,000 homeless assistance programs in 21,000 service locations operating in the United States. Food pantries (about 9,000) were the most common type of program, followed by emergency shelters (about 5,700), transitional housing programs (about 4,400), soup kitchens (about 3,500), outreach programs (about 3,300), and voucher distribution programs (about 3,100). Nonprofit agencies operated 85% of all homeless assistance programs; 51% were operated by secular non-profits and 34% were operated by faith-based nonprofits. Government agencies operated only 14% of homeless assistance programs.

The Federal Response to Homelessness

Before the early 1980s, most homeless assistance took place at the local level. However, as advocates for the homeless achieved national attention for the problem of modern homelessness, the federal government played a greater role in responding to homelessness. In 1983, the first federal task force was created to provide information to local governments and other parties on how to obtain surplus federal property that could be used for providing shelter and other services for the homeless. On June 26, 1986, H.R. 5140 and S. 2608 were introduced as the Homeless Persons' Survival Act to provide a comprehensive aid package for homeless persons. No further action was taken on either measure. However, later that same year, legislation containing Title I of the Homeless Persons' Survival Act — emergency relief provisions for shelter, food, mobile health care, and transitional housing — was introduced as the Urgent Relief for the Homeless Act (H.R. 5710). The legislation passed both houses of Congress in 1987 with large bipartisan majorities. The act was renamed the Stewart B. McKinney Homeless Assistance Act[7] after the death of its chief sponsor, Stewart B. McKinney of Connecticut. President Ronald Reagan signed the act into law on July 22, 1987 (P.L. 100-77).

The original McKinney Act consisted of 15 programs providing an array of services for the homeless. The act also established the Interagency Council on the Homeless, which is designed to provide guidance on the federal response to homelessness through the coordination of the efforts of multiple federal agencies covered under the McKinney Act. Since the enactment of the McKinney-Vento Homeless Assistance Act, there have been several legislative changes to programs and services provided under the act. Specific programs covered under the McKinney-Vento Act, as well as other federal programs responding to homeless, are discussed below.

Department of Education (ED)

Education for Homeless Children and Youth (42 U.S.C. §§ 11431-11435)
      This program is authorized under Title VII, Part B, of the McKinney-Vento Homeless Assistance Act; it assists state education agencies (SEAs) to ensure that all homeless children and youth have equal access to the same free, appropriate public education, including public preschool education, that is provided to other children and youth. Grants made by SEAs to local education agencies (LEAs) under this program must be used to facilitate the enrollment, attendance, and success in school of homeless children and youth. The LEAs may use the funds for activities such as tutoring, supplemental instruction, and referral services for homeless children and youth, as well as providing them with medical, dental, mental, and other health services. In order to receive funds, each state must submit a plan indicating how homeless children and youth will be identified, how assurances will be put in place that homeless children will participate in federal, state, and local food programs if eligible, and how the state will address such problems as transportation, immunization, residency requirements, and the lack of birth certificates or school records.
      Education for Homeless Children and Youth grants are allotted to SEAs in proportion to grants made under Title I, Part A of the Elementary and Secondary Education Act of 1965, except that no state can receive less than the greater of $150,000, 0.25% of the total annual appropriation, or the amount received in FY2001 under this program. The Department of Education must reserve 0.1% of the total appropriation in order to provide grants to outlying areas (Virgin Islands, Guam, American Samoa, and the Commonwealth of the Northern Mariana Islands). The Department also must transfer 1.0% of the total appropriation to the Department of the Interior for Bureau of Indian Affairs services to homeless children and youth.
      The No Child Left Behind Act of 2001 (P.L. 107-110) amended the program explicitly to prohibit states that receive McKinney-Vento funds from segregating homeless students from non-homeless students, except for

short periods of time for health and safety emergencies or to provide temporary, special, supplementary services. An exception was made for four counties that operated separate schools for homeless students in FY2000 (San Joaquin, Orange, and San Diego counties in California, and Maricopa County in Arizona), as long as those separate schools offered services that are comparable to local schools and homeless children were not required to attend them. The Education for Homeless Children and Youth Program is authorized, under P.L. 107-110, through FY2007 at 42 U.S.C. §11435, as amended. No significant legislative changes for the program are anticipated before the 110th Congress.

Department of Homeland Security (DHS)

Emergency Food and Shelter Program (EFSP) (42 U.S.C. §§ 11331-11352)

The EFSP is administered by the Emergency Preparedness and Response Directorate, also referred to as the Federal Emergency Management Agency (FEMA), in the Department of Homeland Security, and is governed by a National Board chaired by FEMA. The Board includes representatives from the United Way of America, the Salvation Army, the National Council of Churches of Christ in the U.S.A., Catholic Charities U.S.A., the Council of Jewish Federations and the American Red Cross. The United Way of America was selected as the secretariat and fiscal agent to perform necessary administrative duties for the board. The National Board establishes written guidelines each year which are published, when modified, in the *Federal Register*. Each area designated by the National Board to receive funds for that year must convene a local board. The Local Board determines which private nonprofit or public organizations of the local government within individual localities should receive grants to act as service providers. Affiliates of the organizations represented on the National Board are invited to join the local board if possible; if a selected jurisdiction is part of an Indian reservation, the board must include a Native American. Also, all local boards must include a homeless or a formerly homeless person.

EFSP funds can be used for food banks/pantries, mass shelters (five or more beds), mass feeding sites, emergency repairs to meet building codes of mass feeding facilities or shelters, limited emergency rent or mortgage assistance and limited utility assistance for individuals or families to prevent homelessness.

The EFSP was established by the Temporary Emergency Food Assistance Act of 1983 (P.L. 98-8); in 1987 it was authorized under the McKinney-Vento Homeless Assistance Act. The authorization for the EFSP expired at the end of FY1994 (42 U.S.C. §11352); however, it continues to be funded through annual appropriations.

Department of Health and Human Services (HHS)

Health Care for the Homeless (HCH) Program (42 U.S.C. §254b(h)
This program is authorized as a Health Center Program under the Public Health Service Act and is administered by the Health Resources and Services Administration (HRSA). The program provides funds to 159 grantees for health centers to provide health services to a special medically underserved population comprised of homeless individuals. Grants are also available for innovative programs that provide outreach and comprehensive primary health services to homeless children and children at risk of homelessness. Centers that receive grants to care for the homeless are required to provide substance abuse treatment as a condition of the grant. In CY2003, approximately 569,000 homeless individuals were provided services by the HCH program. This program is authorized through FY2006 at 42 U.S.C. §254b(j)(6). For more information, see CRS Report RL32046, *Federal Health Centers Program*, by Sharon Coleman.

Projects for Assistance in Transition from Homelessness (PATH) (42 U.S.C. §290cc-21 through 290cc-35)
The PATH program supports a wide network of state and local agencies that provide community-based outreach, mental health, substance abuse, case management and other support services in a variety of settings for people with serious mental health illness (including those with co-occurring substance abuse disorders) who are homeless or at risk of becoming homeless. The PATH program provides these services through formula grants of at least $300,000 to each state, the District of Columbia, and Puerto Rico. The U.S. territories each receive $50,000. States must provide matching funds of at least $1 for every $3 of federal funds. In FY2003, states exceeded the minimum level of matching funds, providing more than $30.3 million in funds to match the $41.3 million in federal funding. Up to 20% of the federal payments may be used for housing subsidies and other services to help individuals access housing resources. The PATH program is authorized under Title V of the Public Health Service Act (Sections 521 — 535) and

administered by the Center for Mental Health Services within the Substance Abuse and Mental Health Services Administration (SAMHSA). Authorization for the PATH program expired at the end of FY2003; however, it continues to be funded through annual appropriations. For more information go to [http://pathprogram. samhsa.gov].

Consolidated Runaway and Homeless Youth Program

This program was initially authorized as the Runaway and Homeless Youth Program under Title III, Runaway and Homeless Youth Act (RHYA), of the Juvenile Justice and Delinquency Prevention Act, amended, (JJDPA, P.L. 93-415). The program is administered by the Family and Youth Services Bureau (FYSB) within the Administration for Children and Families. In October 1999, the Missing, Exploited, and Runaway Children Protection Act (MERCPA) reauthorized RHYA through FY2003 (42 U.S.C. §5751), consolidated funding for its program components —Basic Center Program (BCP) and Transitional Living Program (TLP) — and renamed the program as the Consolidated Runaway and Homeless Youth Program. On October 10, 2003, the Runaway, Homeless, and Missing Children Protection Act was signed into law (P.L. 108-96) reauthorizing and amending RHYA and the Missing Children's Assistance Act for FY2004 through FY2008. RHYA mandates that 90% of appropriated funds be used for BCP and TLP for creating and operating community-based runaway and homeless youth centers and shelters. The reauthorized law, however, adjusts the percentage split for BCP and TLP funding by increasing the TLP minimum to 45% (of the 90% funding required for the BCP and TLP projects) and allows this percentage to be increased up to 55% for those fiscal years when continuation grants are obligated and the quality or number of applicants for both BCP and TLP warrant such an adjustment. The remaining 10% of the funds must be used for a national communications system — that is, the National Runaway Switchboard, which is the national toll free runaway and homeless youth crisis hotline, an information clearinghouse; training and technical assistance activities; research and demonstration projects that seek to improve program administration; and outreach through prevention activities. For more detail, see CRS Report RL31933, *The Runaway and Homeless Youth Program: Administration, Funding, and Legislative Actions*, by Edith Fairman Cooper.

Basic Center Program (42 U.S.C. §§5701-5751)

The purpose of the Basic Center Program is to meet the immediate needs of runaway and homeless youth and their families through creating or strengthening local community-based programs. The goals of BCP are to lighten the problems of such youth; reunite them with their families, and promote resolving family problems through counseling and other avenues; reinforce family connections and foster a stable home life; and help such youth to make constructive decisions regarding their plight. Grants are awarded to local public and nonprofit private organizations, and a combination of such groups to establish and operate local runaway and homeless youth centers, unless they are components of the law enforcement framework or the juvenile justice system. Grants are used to develop or strengthen community-based centers that are outside the law enforcement, juvenile justice, child welfare and mental health systems. Grants are allotted among the states using a formula based on the population of persons under age 18 in each state, proportionate to the national population of youth under age 18. The eligible organizations apply directly to the federal government and compete for BCP grants, subject to the state allotments. Priority is given to applicants who have demonstrated experience in providing services to runaway and homeless youth. Grants are awarded generally for a three-year project period. Funding for subsequent second and third year periods depends on satisfactory performance as well as the availability of funds. Shelter is offered to youth who are younger than 18 years of age and to those who are at risk of separation from their family. Also, BCP must provide age appropriate services or referrals for 18- to 21-year-old homeless youth. Grantees are required to submit semiannual financial and program reports, as well as a final report 90 days after the end of the project period.

Transitional Living Program. (42 U.S.C. §§5714-1 through 5714-2)
     The Transitional Living Program assists older homeless youth (16- to 21-year-olds), including pregnant and parenting youth, who need longer-term supportive assistance.
     Services are geared toward assuring such youth a successful transition to independent self-sufficiency and avoidance of long-term dependence on social services. Grants are available to states, local units of government, a combination of such units, public or private nonprofit agencies, organizations, institutions or other nonprofit entities, faith-based organizations, federally recognized or unrecognized Indian tribes, and to urban Indian tribes. TLP services cannot exceed 18 months, unless participating youth are younger than 18. In such cases, those persons may remain in the program for an additional 180 days (that is, six months) or until they reach the age of 18, whichever occurs first. The program provides shelter — such as group homes, host family homes, and supervised

apartments — and services — including information and counseling services in basic life skills (which include money management, budgeting, consumer education, and use of credit), interpersonal skill building, educational advancement, job attainment skills, and mental and physical health care to runaway and homeless teens. TLP grants are awarded competitively for five year project periods. Grantees are required to provide non-federal matching funds that are equal to at least 10% of the federal share. The non-federal share can be provided through cash or in-kind contributions. Grantees are encouraged, however, to provide cash contributions. Also, grantees must submit semiannual progress and fiscal reports, and a final program and expenditure report within 90 days after the project period is completed.

Maternity Group Homes. For FY2002, the Bush Administration proposed a Maternity Group Home Initiative as part of the Runaway and Homeless Youth Program's TLP component. Maternity group homes (MGH) would provide a supportive and supervised living arrangement for unwed teen mothers (16 to 21) and their children. Such mothers would be provided transitional living guidance, including lessons on parenting, child development, health and nutrition, and other skills. The goal would be to promote the long-term economic independence of unwed teen mothers in order to ensure the well-being of their children. For each of FY2003 through FY2006, the President has requested $10 million for MGH. To date, Congress, however, has not appropriated any specific funding for MGH. Grantees may and do use TLP funds to directly serve unwed pregnant and parenting teens, without a specific set-aside. For more information, see CRS Report RL31540, *Second Chance Homes: Federal Funding, Programs, and Services*, by Edith Fairman Cooper.

Runaway and Homeless Youth — Street Outreach Program.[8] (42 U.S.C. §5712d)

Congressional concern about possible sexual abuse and exploitation of runaway and homeless youth living on the streets led to creating the Street Outreach Program through the Violence Against Women Act of the Violent Crime Control and Law Enforcement Act of 1994 (P.L. 103-332). MERCPA amended RHYA to include the Street Outreach Program as a separately-funded program component. SOP, which also is administered by FYSB, provides grants to nonprofit groups for street-based outreach and education, including treatment, counseling and referral services for runaway, homeless, and street youth who have been subjected to, or are at risk of being subjected to sexual abuse. SOP staff must have access to local emergency shelter space or such space that can be made available for youth who are willing to leave the streets. Accommodations are needed in order to maintain interaction with such youth during the time that they are in the shelter. Only private, nonprofit agencies are eligible to participate in SOP. Such organizations include federally or nonfederally recognized Indian tribes and urban Indian groups that can apply as private, non-profit agencies. No public agencies are eligible. Priority must be given to eligible agencies that have experience in providing services to runaway, homeless, and street youth. As with BCP awards, SOP grants generally are awarded for three-year project periods. Funding for subsequent second and third year periods depends on satisfactory performance as well as the availability of funds. Like TLP, SOP grantees must provide non-federal matching funds that are equal to at least 10% of the federal share. The non-federal share can be provided through cash or in-kind contributions. Grantees are encouraged, however, to provide cash contributions. Also, grantees are required to submit semiannual progress and fiscal reports, and a final program and expenditure report within 90 days after the project period is completed. For more information, see CRS Report RL31933, *The Runaway and Homeless Youth Program: Administration, Funding, and Legislative Actions*, by Edith Fairman Cooper.

Department of Justice (DOJ)

Transitional Housing Assistance for Victims of Domestic Violence

The Violence Against Women Act of 2000 (VAWA 2000; P.L. 106-386; 42 U.S.C. 10419) amended Title III of the Family Violence Prevention and Services Act (42 U.S.C. 10401 et seq.) to create transitional housing assistance for victims of domestic violence. The Act authorizes the Secretary of the Department of Health and Human Services (HHS) to provide grants to states to assist an eligible individual or dependent, who is either fleeing domestic violence or for whom emergency shelter services are lacking, to find and obtain permanent housing. In addition, the program is designed to help a person become integrated into the community through provision of transportation, counseling, child care services, case management, employment counseling and other assistance. A person or dependent can receive transitional housing assistance for a maximum of 18 months. Authorized funding for the program was $25 million for FY2001. With passage of the Keeping Children and Families Safe Act of 2003 (P.L. 108-36; 42 U.S.C. 10419), Section 319(f) of the Family Violence Prevention and Services Act was amended to reauthorize the transitional housing assistance program for each FY2003 through FY2008. No funding, however, has ever been requested or appropriated for the transitional housing program at HHS.

The 108th Congress passed the Prosecutorial Remedies and Other Tools to End the Exploitation of Children Today Act of 2003 (the PROTECT Act, P.L. 108-21; 42 U.S.C. 13975), which contains provisions that are very similar to the transitional housing assistance program that is authorized to be administered by HHS. The PROTECT Act extends transitional housing assistance to child victims of domestic violence, stalking, or sexual assault. The Act provides for the *Department of Justice* to administer this transitional housing assistance grant program. In consultation with the Director of the Violence Against Women Office, the Attorney General provides grants to states, units of local governments, Indian tribes, and other organizations to help eligible persons who need temporary housing. Under the PROTECT Act, transitional housing assistance can be provided for a maximum of 24 months. Authorization for the program is $30 million for each of FY2004 through FY2008. Funding was requested and has been provided for each of FY2004 and FY2005. (For additional information, see CRS Report RL30871, *Violence Against Women Act: History and Federal Funding,* by Garrine P. Laney.)

Department of Housing and Urban Development (HUD)

Homeless Assistance Grants

The Homeless Assistance Grants account was established to provide funding for HUD's four major grants programs that fund housing and services for the homeless. Funding for the Emergency Shelter Grants program is allocated to states and localities on a formula basis. Funding for the three competitive programs — Supportive Housing Program (SHP), Shelter Plus Care Program (S+C), Section 8 Moderate Rehabilitation Assistance for Single-Room Occupancy Dwellings (SRO) — is disseminated through HUD's Continuum of Care (CoC) system. Under the CoC strategy, local communities establish CoC coordinating boards made up of local government and service providers. The CoC boards establish local priorities and strategies to address homelessness in their communities. Local programs that wish to receive HUD funding submit their applications to the CoC boards, which then review them, prioritize them, and submit them to HUD for review. Under HUD's CoC strategy, localities and states are encouraged to develop and maintain assistance systems which integrate programs and services for the homeless or potentially homeless. Out of concern that not enough CoC dollars were being spent on housing, since FY2002, Congress has required that not less than 30% of funds appropriated to the Homeless Assistance Grants programs be used for permanent housing and that all funding for services be matched at a 25% rate.

There has been variation in the programs funded under the homeless assistance grants since HUD consolidated its homeless programs in 1995. For example, for the first several years, HUD consolidated seven McKinney-Vento Act homeless assistance programs under this grant — Shelter Plus Care, Supportive Housing, Emergency Shelter Grants, Section 8 Moderate Rehabilitation (Single Room Occupancy), Rural Homeless Grants, and Safe Havens for Homeless Individuals, as well as the Innovative Homeless Initiatives Demonstration Program. Rural Homeless Grants and Safe Havens for Homeless Individuals still exist statutorily, although they have not been funded for years. The following is a description of the four programs that are presently funded under the homeless assistance grants.

Supportive Housing Program (SHP). (42 U.S.C. §§11381-11389)

This competitive grant program was created by the McKinney-Vento Homeless Assistance Act of 1987, as amended. Housing funded under SHP may be transitional within a 24-month period, permanent housing for the disabled, or a single room occupancy dwelling. In order to receive funds, permanent housing must provide supportive services for its residents such as case management, child care, employment assistance, outpatient health services, food and cash assistance and assistance in obtaining permanent housing. States, local governmental entities, private nonprofit organizations, or community mental health associations that are public nonprofit organizations may apply for funds through their local CoC board.

This program requires that not less than 25% of appropriated funds be used to serve homeless families with children, not less than 25% be used to serve homeless persons with disabilities, and not less than 10% be used for providing supportive services. There is also a dollar-for-dollar match requirement, and no provider may use more than 5% of SHP funds for administrative purposes. The authorization for this program (42 U.S.C. §11389) expired at the end of FY1994; however, it has continued to be funded through annual appropriations.

Shelter Plus Care Program (S+C). (42 U.S.C. §§11403-11406b)

This program was created by the McKinney-Vento Homeless Assistance Act, as amended. The S+C program provides rental subsidies to homeless adults with disabilities. Similar to the Section 8 program, tenants pay 30% of their income towards housing and the administering body pays the rest. The assistance is funded for five years, but can be renewed at the end of those five years. S+C grants must be matched by local communities dollar for dollar. While S+C grant dollars cannot be used to fund supportive services, grantees are expected to partner with other agencies to provide social services and the dollar for dollar match requirement can be met through spending on services. Not less than 50% of S+C vouchers must be reserved for homeless individuals who are seriously mentally ill, have chronic substance abuse problems, or both. A state, unit of general local government (city, county, town, township, parish, or village) or public housing agency may apply for funds through their local CoC boards. Grantees may provide rental assistance to private nonprofit entities (including community mental health centers established as nonprofit organizations) that own or lease dwelling units. The authorization for this program (42 U.S.C. §11403h) expired at the end of FY1994; however, the program has continued to be funded through annual appropriations.

Funding for S+C contracts is provided in one-year increments, as a result, all S+C subsidies expire and require new funding every year. Unless Congress provides sufficient funding to renew all contracts every year, S+C assistance will expire and homeless families risk losing their assistance. At the end of 2001, 28,500 rent subsidies were being funded through the S+C program. Growth in the program is limited, however, due to the high cost of renewing expiring contracts. Some communities are concerned that the cost of renewing S+C contracts may eventually consume the entire Homeless Assistance Grants funding allocation.

Section 8 Moderate Rehabilitation Assistance for Single-Room Occupancy Dwellings (SRO). (42 U.S.C. §§11407-11407b)

This program was created by the McKinney-Vento Homeless Assistance Act of 1987, as amended, to provide rental assistance to homeless single individuals. Under the program, HUD provides rental subsidies, through public housing agencies, in connection with the moderate rehabilitation of residential properties that contain multiple single room dwelling units. These project units are similar to dormitories, having single bedrooms, community bathrooms, and kitchen facilities. Funds for this program may also come from the *Shelter Plus Care Program*. As of 2001, 9,500 SRO units had been funded under this program. Growth in the SRO program has been severely limited in recent years because of the high upfront cost of 10 year contracts as well as a dwindling supply of eligible buildings. The authorization for this program (42 U.S.C. §11403h) expired at the end of FY1994; however, it has continued to be funded through annual appropriations.

Emergency Shelter Grants Program (ESG). (42 U.S.C. §§11371-11378)

This program was authorized through the McKinney-Vento Homeless Assistance Act, as amended. ESG is a formula grants program to state and local governments (any local government may distribute all or a portion of the funds to private nonprofit organizations providing assistance to homeless individuals). ESG funds are distributed so that state and local governments receive the same proportion of total ESG funds as they receive of total Community Development Block Grant (CDBG) funds. Emergency Shelter Grants are used for the renovation, major rehabilitation or conversion of buildings into emergency shelters. Essential services, including employment, health, drug abuse or education services may also be funded with ESG funds (up to 30% of funds may be used for building renovations and essential services). Maintenance, operation, insurance, utilities and furnishing costs for these emergency shelters may also be funded under this program, although not more than 10% of the funds may be used for staffing costs. To prevent homelessness, financial assistance may be given to families who have received eviction or termination of utility service notices if: (1) the inability to make such payments is due to a sudden reduction in income, (2) there is a reasonable prospect that the family will be able to resume payments within a reasonable period of time, and (3) the assistance will not supplant funding for preexisting homelessness prevention activities from other sources (up to 30% of funds may be used for this activity). There is a one-for-one match requirement for local governments; there is no match requirement for the first $100,000 for states, but a one-for-one match is required for the remainder of the funds. The authorization for this program (42 U.S.C. §11377) expired at the end of FY1994; however, the program has continued to be funded through annual appropriations.

Department of Labor (DOL)

Homeless Veterans Reintegration Program. (38 U.S.C. §2021)

The Homeless Veterans Reintegration Program (HVRP) provides grants to states or other public entities and non-profits, including faith-based organizations, to operate employment programs that reach out to homeless veterans. The main goal of the HVRP is to reintegrate homeless veterans into the economic mainstream and labor force. This program was recodified under veterans benefits by the Homeless Veterans Comprehensive Assistance Act of 2001 (P.L. 107-95); formerly, it was authorized under the McKinney-Vento Homeless Assistance Act of 1987. For FY2003, the Administration proposed to move this program from the Department of Labor (DOL) to the Department of Veterans Affairs (VA), consolidating the program with two other DOL programs, the Disabled Veterans' Outreach Program (DVOP) and the Local Veterans' Employment Representatives (LVER). This consolidation was not undertaken by Congress; and for FY2004 and FY2005, no such plan was proposed by the Administration. However, DVOP and LVER resources are used in projects to support employment efforts under HVRP. This program is authorized at 38 U.S.C. §2021(e) through FY2006 at $50 million per fiscal year. H.R. 2131, discussed later in this report, would reauthorize the program at the same amount through FY2011 and broaden its scope to include veterans at imminent risk of homelessness.

Department of Veterans Affairs (VA)

Health Care for Homeless Veterans (HCHV). [9] (38 U.S.C. §§2031-2034)
This program operates at 76 sites where VA provides outreach services, physical and psychiatric health exams, treatment, referrals, to homeless veterans with mental health problems, including substance abuse. As appropriate, the HCHV program places homeless veterans needing long-term treatment into one of its 200 contract community-based facilities. Residential housing may be purchased or leased with program funds to operate therapeutic transitional housing (38 U.S.C. §§2032, 2042). Under this program, the VA is required to coordinate and provide services in conjunction with state and local governments, other appropriate departments and agencies of the federal government and non-governmental organizations. This program was created by the Hospital, Nursing Home, Domiciliary and Medical Care Act (38 U.S.C. 1710). This program is authorized until December 31, 2006 at 38 U.S.C. §2033. In 2004, VA's 134 HCHV program provided outreach, treatment, and referral services to 64,000 homeless veterans.

Homeless Providers Grant and Per Diem Program.[10] (38 U.S.C. §§2011-2013)

Under this program, grants are awarded to public or private nonprofit organizations to provide outreach, rehabilitative services, vocational counseling and training, and supported housing (38 U.S.C. §2042) to homeless veterans. Funds may be used for the expansion, remodeling, or alteration of existing buildings or the acquisition of facilities for use as service centers, transitional housing or other facilities, and for the procurement of vans for use in outreach to and transportation for, homeless veterans. Service centers must provide health care, mental health services, hygiene facilities, benefits and employment counseling, meals, and transportation assistance. Centers must also be equipped to provide job training, counseling and placement services (including job readiness and literacy and skills training), as well as any outreach and case management services which may be necessary. A grant may not be used to support operational costs. In April 2004, VA announced the award of $15 million in "Per Diem Only" funding to 80 faith-based and community-based agencies which will support 1,583 beds for homeless veterans. Currently 6,463 beds (67%) of the expected 9,600 Grant and Per Diem-funded beds are operational and serving homeless veterans.

Homeless Veterans with Special Needs. (38 U.S.C. §2061)

Within the Homeless Providers Grant and Per Diem program there is also a "special purpose program" which makes $5 million per fiscal year available to provide grants to health care facilities and to grant and per diem providers to encourage the development of programs for homeless veterans who are women (including women who care for minor dependents), frail elderly, terminally ill, or chronically mentally ill.

Domiciliary Care for Homeless Veterans (DCHV). (38 U.S.C. §1710(b))

This program is a residential rehabilitation program specifically intended to meet the clinical needs of homeless veterans while preventing the therapeutically inappropriate use of hospital and nursing home care services. VA operates the DCHV program at 34 locations across the country. A multi-dimensional, individually tailored treatment approach is used and the clinical status of the veteran is stabilized while the underlying causes of homelessness are addressed. The basic components of the DCHV program include community outreach and referral, admission screening and assessment, medical and psychiatric evaluation, treatment and rehabilitation, and post-discharge community support. DCHV staff help veterans apply for housing assistance, or arrangements are made for placement of homeless veterans in long-term care facilities such as State Soldiers Homes, group homes, adult foster care or halfway houses. Homeless veterans are provided employment training through involvement in VA's Incentive Therapy Program, a medically prescribed rehabilitation program involving therapeutic work assignments at VA medical centers for which veterans receive nominal payments. The Homeless Veterans Comprehensive Assistance Act of 2001 (P.L. 107-95) amended the program by authorizing the Secretary of VA to establish up to 10 additional programs to provide domiciliary services to homeless veterans. Although the Act authorized $5 million each for FY2003 and FY2004, no funds were appropriated. The authorization for these additional programs expired at the end of FY2004. VA plans to establish additional domiciliary programs sometime during FY2005 with funds from the medical services budget. In FY2004,VA's existing DCHV programs provided treatment to over 5,000 homeless veterans.

Compensated Work Therapy Program (formerly the Special Therapeutic and Rehabilitation Activities Fund).[11] (38 U.S.C. §2063)

The Compensated Work Therapy (CWT) program is a comprehensive rehabilitation program that prepares veterans for competitive employment and independent living. The major goals of the program are: 1) to use remunerative work to maximize a veteran's level of functioning; 2) to prepare veterans for successful re-entry into the community as productive citizens, and; 3) to provide a structured daily activity to those veterans with severe and chronic disabling physical and/or mental conditions. As part of their work therapy veterans produce items for sale or undertake subcontracts to provide certain products and/or services such as by providing temporary staffing to a company. Funds collected from the sale of these products and/or services were used to fund the program. Funding for this program comes from the VA's Special Therapeutic and Rehabilitation Activities Fund, which is permanently authorized at 38 U.S.C. §1718(c).

Guaranteed Transitional Housing for Homeless Veterans. (38 U.S.C. §§2051-2054)

Qualified nonprofit organizations or other qualified organizations that have experience in underwriting transitional housing projects may obtain a loan under this program for the construction, rehabilitation or acquisition of land for a multifamily transitional housing project. Under this program, housing may be single room occupancy and must provide supportive and counseling services (including job counseling) with the goal of encouraging self-sufficiency among participating veterans. To qualify, a project must require the occupant veteran to seek and maintain employment. The project must also maintain strict guidelines regarding the sobriety of participants. Occupants must pay a reasonable fee in order to live in these transitional units. Veterans who are not homeless and homeless individuals who are not veterans may be occupants of transitional housing if all of the transitional housing needs of homeless veterans in the project area have been met. Not more than 15 loans with an aggregate total up to $100 million may be guaranteed under this program. Funding for this program is authorized as a pilot project at 38 U.S.C. §2051.

Technical Assistance Grants. (38 U.S.C. §2064)

Under this program, VA provides grants to entities with expertise in preparing grant applications. The grantee must then provide technical assistance to nonprofit community-based groups who are applying for grants to assist homeless veterans. This program is authorized through FY2005 at 38 U.S.C. §2064.

HUD VA Supported Housing (HUD-VASH). (42 U.S.C. §1437f (o))

This joint HUD and VA supported housing program provides specially designated HUD rental assistance (Section 8) vouchers to homeless veterans. Every homeless veteran who receives a housing voucher must be assigned to a VA case manager and receive supportive services. This program serves homeless veterans who have chronic mental illnesses or chronic substance abuse disorders. Before a veteran may participate in this program, he or she must agree to continue treatment for the mental illness or substance abuse disorder. Today's HUD VASH program originally began as a Memorandum of Agreement between HUD and the VA and through that relationship, 1,780 vouchers were created and are in circulation today. The Homeless Veterans Comprehensive Assistance Act of 2001 (P.L. 107-95) codified the program and authorized the creation of an additional 500 vouchers each year for FY2003-FY2006. However, HUD has not requested, and Congress has not provided, funds for HUD-VASH vouchers since the program was codified.

Other VA Activities

In addition to the targeted programs for which specific funding is available, as shown in Table 2, the VA engages in several activities to assist the homeless that are not reflected in this report as separate programs. An

Advisory Committee on Homeless Veterans was established within VA (15 members appointed from veterans service organizations, community-based providers of services to homeless individuals, previously homeless veterans, experts in mental illness, substance use disorders and others) to consult with and seek advice concerning VA benefits and services to homeless veterans (38 U.S.C. §2066). A *demonstration program of referral and counseling* serves veterans who are in transition from certain institutions (penal institutions or long-term care mental institutions) and provides information about the benefits and services available to them under the VA programs (38 U.S.C. §2023). VA has several *Comprehensive Homeless Centers (CHCs)* in various cities, which consolidate all of VA's homeless programs in that area into a single organizational framework to promote integration within VA and coordination with non-VA homeless programs. CHCs offer a comprehensive continuum of care (CoC) to help homeless veterans escape from homelessness. VA also sponsors *Drop-in Centers,* which provide a daytime sanctuary where homeless veterans can clean up, wash their clothes, get a daytime meal, and participate in a variety of low intensity therapeutic and rehabilitative activities. Linkages with longer-term assistance are also available. The *VA Excess Property for Homeless Veterans Initiative* provides for the distribution of federal excess personal property (hats, parkas, footwear, sleeping bags) to homeless veterans and homeless veterans programs. VA also operates a pilot project with the Social Security Administration (SSA) called *SSA-VA Outreach* where HCMI and DCHV staff coordinate outreach and benefits certification with SSA staff to increase the number of veterans receiving SSA benefits and otherwise assist in their rehabilitation.

VA programs and staff have actively participated in each of the *Stand Downs for Homeless Veterans* run by local coalitions in various cities each year. Stand Downs give homeless veterans one to three days of safety and security where they can obtain food, shelter, clothing, and a range of other types of assistance, including VA provided health care, benefits certification, and linkages with other programs. In a program called Veterans Benefits Administration (*VBA)'s Acquired Property Sales for Homeless Providers,* VA is able to sell, at a discount, foreclosed properties to nonprofit organizations and government agencies that will use them to shelter or house homeless veterans. This program was reauthorized by P.L. 108-170 through December 31, 2008 (38 U.S.C. §2041). Certain specified homeless veterans are eligible for a one-time course of dental care for homeless veterans engaged in rehabilitation (38 U.S.C. §2062). Finally, *Project CHALENG for Veterans,* is a nationwide VA initiative in which VA's Community

Homelessness Assessment Local Education and Networking Groups work with other federal agencies, state and local governments, and nonprofit organizations to assess the needs of homeless veterans and develop action plans to meet identified needs.

ADMINISTRATION INITIATIVES AND LEGISLATION IN THE 109TH CONGRESS

Administration Initiatives

The Chronic Homelessness Initiative

The Bush Administration has established a national goal of ending chronic homelessness in 10 years, by 2012. The idea of a 10-year plan to end *chronic* homelessness began as a part of a 10-year plan to end homelessness *in general* adopted by the National Alliance to End Homelessness (NAEH) in 2000. The following year, then-Secretary Martinez announced HUD's commitment to ending chronic homelessness at the NAEH annual conference. In 2002, as a part of his FY2003 budget, President Bush made "ending chronic homelessness in the next decade a top objective." The bi-partisan, congressionally-mandated, Millennial Housing Commission, in its Report to Congress in 2002, included ending chronic homelessness in 10 years among its principal recommendations. By 2003, the Interagency Council on Homelessness had been re-engaged[12] and charged with pursuing the President's 10-year plan. During 2004, several major cities (including New York and the District of Columbia) committed themselves to the goal of ending chronic homelessness in 10 years.

The Interagency Council on Homelessness has adopted a working definition to identify the chronically homeless; a chronically homeless individual is "an unaccompanied homeless individual with a disabling condition who has been either continually homeless for a year or has had at least four episodes of homelessness in the past three years." Part of the reason behind the focus on the chronically homeless is the estimate that the chronically homeless account for about 10% of all users of the homeless shelter system, but that they use 50% of the total days of shelter provided.[13]

While the chronically homeless may monopolize current resources, some advocates for the homeless and the Administration argue that there are better ways to serve them. Permanent supportive housing is generally seen as the solution to ending chronic homelessness.[14] Permanent supportive housing consists of low-cost housing, partnered with social services, available to low-income and/or homeless households. Services can include case management, substance abuse counseling, mental health services, income management and support, and life skills services. Not only has supportive housing proven to be effective, studies have also argued that it is cost efficient. By housing the chronically homeless in permanent supportive housing, they are less likely to be housed temporarily by more expensive public services, such as emergency room services and jail or even prison.[15] The Millennial Housing Commission's final report supported this finding, stating that "the chronically homeless require permanent supportive housing to escape and reduce the enormous burden on public care systems."

The goal of ending chronic homelessness has gained wide support and prominence in a short time. However, some advocates for the homeless are concerned about the focus on the chronically homeless. In particular, they feel that the initiative does not work to solve the real problems behind homelessness, which are a lack of affordable housing, health care and income supports. They argue that while these targeted homeless assistance programs may help to stabilize people who are currently homeless, they do nothing to prevent future homelessness among low-income people with or without disabilities. They are also concerned that the focus on a single, disabled population limits the resources available for families, children and other non-disabled populations whose needs may also be great. They disagree that the chronically homeless are necessarily the most needy, especially in rural and suburban areas where street homelessness is less prevalent and that it is inappropriate to pit needy populations against each other for limited resources. Finally, they argue that earmarking resources for the chronically homeless takes away local flexibility to determine local needs and priorities and happens especially at the expense of rural and suburban communities.[16]

The Administration has recently undertaken some collaborative efforts to reach its goal of ending chronic homelessness in 10 years. On October 1, 2003, the Administration announced the award of over $48 million in grants aimed at serving the needs of the chronically homeless through two initiatives. The *"Ending Chronic Homelessness through Employment and Housing"* initiative was a collaborative grant offered jointly by HUD and the Department of Labor (DOL). The initiative offered $10 million from HUD and $3.5 million from DOL to help the chronically homeless in five communities gain access to employment and permanent housing. The *"Collaborative Initiative to Help End Chronic Homelessness"* was a $35 million grant initiative offered jointly by HUD, HHS, and VA. Specifically, $20 million was available in HUD funds to provide permanent housing under the SHP, S+C, or SRO programs; $7 million was available through HHS's Substance Abuse and Mental Health Services Agency (SAMHSA) to fund substance abuse treatment and mental health and related social services for the chronically homeless; $3 million was available through HHS's Health Resources and Services Administration (HRSA) to provide primary care for the chronically homeless; and $5 million in additional resources were made available at local VA hospitals for serving homeless veterans.

Homeless Assistance Grants Funding and Proposed Consolidation

The President's FY2006 budget proposes to consolidate HUD's three competitive programs — *Supportive Housing (SHP), Shelter Plus Care (S+C), and Section 8, Moderate Rehabilitation Assistance for Single-Room Occupancy Dwellings (SRO)* — into one competitive grant program. The Homeless Assistance Grants program would continue to reserve an estimated $150 million for the formula Emergency Shelter Grants program. The HUD budget indicates that the consolidation of the three competitive programs would have significantly streamlined homeless assistance in the United States. A similar consolidation proposal was made for FY2003, FY2004, and FY2005. However, legislation to implement these changes, as well as the reauthorization of the HUD portion of the McKinney-Vento Act, was not introduced or enacted in the past three years and has not been introduced in the 109th Congress. The Administration's funding request for the Homeless Assistance Grants account includes $200 million that would be set aside for a Samaritan Housing Initiative designed to specifically address the supportive housing needs of chronically homeless individuals. Legislation to enact a separate Samaritan Initiative program was introduced but not enacted in the 108th Congress. The request also includes $25 million for a four year Prisoner Re-Entry Initiative to help individuals exiting prison make a successful transition to community life and long-term employment. The funds would be transferred to the Department of Justice. Funding for the Prisoner Re-Entry Initiative was also requested in FY2005, but was not enacted.

Legislative Activities in the 109th Congress

The Services for Ending Long-Term Homelessness Act (H.R. 1471/S.709) was introduced in both the House and the Senate on April 5,

2005. The bi-partisan bill would establish a grant program for services in supportive housing for the chronically homeless. The program would be housed in the Department of Health and Human Services (RRS) and administered by the Substance Abuse and Mental Health Services Administration (SAMHSA). States, cities, public, or nonprofit entities would be eligible to apply and grant funds could be used for services including mental health services, substance abuse treatment, referrals for primary health care and dental services, health education, money management, and parental skills training. The program would require initial grantees to provide $1 for every $3 of federal money and renewal grantees to provide $1 for every $1 of federal money. The bill has been referred to the House Energy and Commerce, Subcommittee on Health and Senate Health, Education, Labor, and Pensions Committee.

The New GI Bill of Rights for the 21st Century (H.R. 2131), introduced on May 5, 2005, is a comprehensive bill to improve benefits for veterans, active duty, and reserve members of the Armed Forces. Subtitle C of title V would reauthorize the Homeless Veterans Reintegration Program at $50 million a year through FY2011 and broaden its scope to include veterans at imminent risk of homelessness. The legislation was referred to the House Veterans' Affairs, House Ways and Means, and House Armed Services committees.

Funding

Table 1 shows final appropriation levels for FY2001-FY2005 for all of the targeted homeless programs included in this report except for programs administered by the VA. Unless otherwise noted, the appropriations figures come from the budget justifications submitted by the various agencies or congressional appropriations documents.

Table 2 shows actual and estimated obligations for the Department of Veterans Affairs targeted homeless programs for FY2001-FY2005. With the exception of the Loan Guaranty Transitional Housing for Homeless Veterans, funding for VA activities described below were not specified as line items in VA appropriations. VA's Loan Guaranty Transitional Housing for Homeless Veterans program began in FY1999; the law allocated $48.25 million for the subsidy for guaranteed loans for transitional housing to remain available until expended. The figures in Table 2 were obtained from both VA budget documents and conversations with VA employees.

Table 1. Homelessness: Targeted Federal Programs Appropriations, FY2002-FY2006 ($ in thousands)

Program	Agencies	FY2002	FY2003	FY2004	FY2005	FY2006 request
Education for Homeless Children & Youth	ED	50,000	54,642	59,646	62,496	62,496
Emergency Food & Shelter (EFSP)	DHS/ FEMA	140,000	153,000	152,000	153,000	153,000
Health Care for the Homeless (HCH)[a]	HHS	116,000	126,621	135,675	145,000	163,000
Projects for Assistance in Transition from Homelessness (PATH)	HHS	39,855	43,073	49,760	54,809	54,809
Consolidated Runaway, Homeless Youth Program	HHS	88,024	89,977	89,431	88,725	88,728
— *Runaway and Homeless Youth - Basic Center*		*48,288*	*49,473*	*49,171*	*48,786*	*48,787*
— *Runaway and Homeless Youth - Transitional Living*		*39,736*	*40,504*	*40,260*	*39,939*	*39,941*
— *Runaway and Homeless Youth - Maternity Group Homes*		—	—	—	—	*10,000*
Runaway and Homeless Youth - Street Outreach Program	HHS	14,999	15,399	15,302	15,178	15,179
Homeless Assistance Grants (HAG)	HUD	1,123,000	1,130,000	1,257,400	1,240,511	1,440,000
Homeless Veterans Reintegration Project	DOL	17,500	18,250	18,888	20,832	22,000
Transitional Housing Assistance for Child Victims of Domestic Violence, Stalking, or Sexual Assault	DOJ	—	—	—	$14,840[b]	$12,300b

Source: Table prepared by the Congressional Research Service (CRS). Unless otherwise stated, sources of data were agency budget justifications and congressional appropriations documents.

Notes: (1) Italics indicate amount is subsumed under earlier line item.

a. This program is funded under the Health Resources and Services Administration (HRSA), Community Health Centers program. The HCH program generally receives about 8% of the funds appropriated for the CHC program.

b. This funding is a set-aside under the VAWA STOP grant program.

Table 2. Homelessness: Targeted VA Program Obligations, FY2002-FY2006 ($ in thousands)

Program	FY2002 (actual)	FY2003 (actual)	FY2004 (actual)	FY2005 (estimate)	FY2006 (estimate)
Health Care for Homeless Veterans (HCHV)[a]	$54,135	$45,188	$42,905	$43,305	$48,705
Homeless Providers Grants and Per Diem Program	22,431	43,388	62,965	86,000	99,000
Domiciliary Care for Homeless Veterans (DCHV)	45,443	49,213	51,829	58,643	60,521
Compensated Work Therapy/Therapeutic Residence Program (CWT/TR)	8,028	8,349	10,240	10,598	10,969
Guaranteed Transitional Housing for Homeless Veterans	528	594	600	22,274	15,776
HUD VA Supported Housing (HUD-VASH)	$4,729	$4,603	$3,375	$3,493	$3,615

Source: Table prepared by the Congressional Research Service (CRS). Data supplied by the Department of Veterans Affairs (VA).

a. Includes funding for the Homeless Chronically Mentally Ill Veterans (HCMI) and the Homeless Comprehensive Service Centers, including mobile centers. A specific breakdown of obligations among activities is not available.

REFERENCES

[1] 42 U.S.C. §11302

[2] See: *HUD Report to Congress: Fourth Progress Report on HUD's Strategy for Improving Homeless Data Collection, Reporting, and Analysis.* Available at [http://www.huduser.org].

[3] A copy may be obtained from the USCM website, at [http://www.
     usmayors.org].

[4] The 2004 cities surveyed were: Boston, Burlington, Cedar Rapids,
     Charleston, Charlotte, Chicago, Cleveland, Denver, Detroit, Kansas
     City, Louisville, Los Angeles, Miami, Nashville, New Orleans, Norfolk,
     Philadelphia, Phoenix, Portland, Providence, St. Paul, Salt Lake City,
     San Antonio, San Francisco, Santa Monica, Seattle, and Trenton.

[5] A   copy   may   be   obtained   from   the   HUD   website,   at
     [http://www.huduser.org]. Click on "Publications," then click on
     "Homelessness."

[6] The federal agencies are Departments of Housing and Urban
     Development; Health and Human Services; Veterans Affairs;
     Agriculture; Commerce; Education; Energy; Justice; Labor;
     Transportation; Social Security Administration; and the Federal
     Emergency Management Agency.

[7] P.L. 106-400 (signed into law on Oct. 30, 2000) renamed the Stewart B.
     McKinney Homeless Assistance Act as the McKinney-Vento Homeless
     Assistance Act.

[8] This program is also known as the Education and Prevention Services to
     Reduce Sexual Abuse of Runaway, Homeless, and Street Youth
     Program.

[9] Formerly called the Homeless Chronically Mentally Ill Veterans
     (HCMI) program.

[10] Formerly called the Homeless Veterans Comprehensive Services
     Programs.

[11] The program was created by the Veterans Omnibus Health Care Act of
     1976 (P.L. 94-581).

[12] ICH was created in 1987 in the Stewart B. McKinney Homeless
     Assistance Act. Its mission is to coordinate the national response to
     homelessness. The ICH is composed of the directors of 18 federal
     departments and agencies whose policies and programs have some
     responsibility for homeless services, including HUD, HHS, the
     Department of Labor (DOL), and the VA. The council was inactive for
     six years, but began receiving funding again in FY2002.

[13] See *Ending Chronic Homelessness: Strategies for Action, Department
     of Health and Human Services,* Report from the Secretary's Work
     Group on Ending Chronic Homelessness, Mar. 2003.

[14] Ibid.

[15] See Dennis Culhane, Stephen Metraux, and Trevor Hadley, "Public
     Service Reductions Associated with Placement of Homeless Persons

with Severe Mental Illness in Supportive Housing," *Housing Policy Debate,* vol. 13, no. 1 (Washington, DC: Fannie Mae Foundation, 2002).

[16] See National Coalition for the Homeless, *Questions and Answers About the "Chronic Homelessness Initiative,"* available at [http://www.nationalhomeless.org/chronic/ chronicqanda.html].

In: Homelessness
Editor: Ernest Todd, pp. 31-131

Chapter 2

STRATEGIES FOR REDUCING CHRONIC STREET HOMELESSNESS[*]

Martha R. Burt[2], John Hedderson[1],
Janine Zweig[2], Mary Jo Orti[1],
Laudan Aron-Turnham[2] and Sabrina M. Johnson[1]
[1] Walter R. McDonald & Associates, Inc. (WRMA) Sacramento, CA
[2] The Urban Institute (UI) Washington, DC

INTRODUCTION

Why This Study Is Important

Today's recognition of homelessness as a social problem is about two decades old. First responses were to treat the problem as an emergency situation. Policy evolved over the years to include recognition that many of the people finding themselves homeless would need more than an emergency bed for a few nights, weeks, or even months to get themselves back into regular housing. Some communities began as early as the late 1990s to reorient themselves toward *ending* either chronic homelessness or all homelessness, and to establish action steps and a time frame in which to do so.

---

[*] Excerpted from Final Report prepared for U.S. Department of Housing and Urban Development, Office of Policy Development and Research dated January 2004.

At its national conference in July 2000, the National Alliance to End Homelessness unveiled a ten-year plan to end homelessness altogether. A significant part of that plan is a blueprint to end *chronic* homelessness in the same time frame. The plan drew on evaluations that show we know how to create programs and supportive services to bring people in off the streets and help them retain housing, and on research that estimates the number of chronically homeless people to be few enough (between 150,000 and 250,000) to make a reasonable target for a successful policy. Two years later, additional research (Culhane, Metraux, and Hadley, 2002) showed that the policy might be close to cost-neutral in public monies as well. Since 2000, this goal of ending chronic homelessness has expanded dramatically. By 2003 the President had endorsed it and reinvigorated the Interagency Council on the Homeless to guide and coordinate the efforts of Federal agencies. Two *New York Times* lead editorials argued forcefully for that goal, the U. S. Conference of Mayors had adopted it, and more than 100 cities and states around the country had committed themselves to developing plans that would make it a reality.

These plans usually have at least two aspects—helping chronically homeless people leave homelessness for good by establishing permanent supportive housing or other supportive networks, and stopping the flow of people likely to experience chronic homelessness by offering housing and appropriate supports for vulnerable people leaving institutions such as substance abuse treatment, psychiatric, or correctional facilities.

This is an experimental time for programs to reduce chronic street homelessness. The many communities that have resolved to end chronic homelessness have to learn about successful approaches,[5] construct their own strategies, and locate the necessary resources to fulfill their plans. These communities can benefit from the experiences of homeless service providers who have been willing and able to participate in developing and implementing new approaches. Given the scope of what needs to be done, integrated community-wide approaches hold the most promise of succeeding.

HUD sponsored this project to identify and describe community-wide approaches that are working in cities around the country.[6] We selected seven communities that were reputed to have made progress in reducing their chronic street homeless population and would be able to document that progress. After conducting site visits, we found that only three of the seven have developed a true community-wide paradigm, but that each of the seven communities had noteworthy strategies that were working to reduce chronic street homelessness. We also discovered common elements in the seven communities' approaches that appear to maximize progress. This report describes these common elements and their role in approaches to reducing chronic street homelessness. Communities just beginning to develop their own plans for reducing chronic homelessness should be able to find illustrative practices and programs that they can learn from and adapt to their own situations.

We found that the most successful of the study communities had experienced a paradigm shift that changed the goals and approaches of their homeless assistance network. This was especially powerful when combined with having a clear goal of reducing chronic street homelessness, a community-wide level of organization, strong leadership and effective organizational structure, and significant resources from mainstream public agencies. These and other key elements are described in detail in Chapter 2. The other chapters in the body of the report describe how the study communities implemented their strategies. The last chapter describes policy, practice, and research implications.

The site visit appendices provide descriptions of how the elements operate together in each of the study communities. These appendices also include site contact information for practices of potential interest to other jurisdictions. None of the study communities have achieved the final goal of ending chronic homelessness, but all provide examples of useful strategies. A few of our study communities have a more complete approach than the others, but all of them are working on improvements.

Purpose of the Research

This project's aim was to identify successful community-wide approaches to reducing homelessness and achieving stable housing for the disabled, difficult-to-serve people who routinely live on the streets, and to document these successful approaches in a way that will help other communities trying to address this problem. We included as "street homeless" single adults who spend significant time on the streets, although they may also use emergency shelters from time to time. Most of the people to be helped will also be "chronically" homeless, which we defined, as does the Interagency Council on the Homeless, as being disabled and either being continuously homeless for a year or more or having had at least four homeless episodes during the last three years. We use the phrase "chronically street homeless" in describing those single adults who meet both criteria. To be successful at the task of reducing chronic homelessness, community approaches must address disabilities such as severe and persistent mental illness, severe and persistent alcohol and/or drug abuse problems, and HIV/AIDS. For succinctness of writing, often in this report we will simply use the terms "chronic homelessness" and "chronically homeless individuals" in referring to the people who are the focus of our inquiry.

This study sought to answer several questions about strategies that communities use to reduce chronic street homelessness:

- Does the community have a long-term plan for reducing/preventing chronic homelessness? What is its approach and what are the elements? What led to this approach and how was it identified? What needs of which homeless people does it address?
- How was the approach implemented? What challenges were encountered? What opportunities were used?
- How is the approach administered and coordinated? What is the role of each stakeholder?
- How is the approach funded? Do requirements of the funding sources create any barriers or promote any successes?
- Did implementation include efforts to reduce local resistance by including community members? How? How successful have these efforts been?
- Can the community document its progress; either by showing that the numbers of street homeless people have decreased or by showing that programs are accepting this population and helping them leave homelessness?
- How else do communities use data to bolster their case for making the investment to end chronic street homelessness?

Who, What, Where, and When

In 2002, HUD contracted with Walter R. McDonald Associates, Inc. and its subcontractor, the Urban Institute, to conduct a study to answer the research questions. HUD asked us to find community-wide approaches to reducing chronic street homelessness, to the extent possible, because its analysts suspected that such a focused commitment might be necessary for substantial progress.

We sought communities appropriate for site visits through recommendations of key informants and a literature search for evaluated projects, identifying over 120 possible programs and communities. Screening phone calls to community and program representatives helped us identify appropriate communities to visit. Criteria for selection included that the community *have* an approach to ending chronic street homelessness, that it be *community-wide,*[7] and that there be *evidence* to document that the approach actually succeeded in reducing chronic street homelessness. (The selection methods are described further in Appendix H.)

We were able to find three communities that met all three criteria, and several others that met the criteria but only for specific subpopulations such as veterans, people with severe mental illness, or people with co-occurring disorders. We also visited four communities that did not meet all criteria. We reasoned that many communities throughout the country would benefit from knowing what could be accomplished even without a community-wide approach, as not all communities will be able to begin with community-wide commitment. The seven communities visited were:

- Birmingham, Alabama;
- Boston, Massachusetts;
- Columbus, Ohio;

Three projects in Los Angeles, California—one focused on homeless veterans, one focused on mentally ill offenders in the county jail system, and one focused on chronic street homeless people in the downtown "Skid Row" area;

- Philadelphia, Pennsylvania;
- San Diego, California; and
- Seattle, Washington.

We conducted site visits to each of these communities, ranging in length from 2 to 5 days depending on the complexity of the community's approach and the components we chose as the focus of our visits. We interviewed between 40 and 90 people per site, including focus groups at each site of 5 to 10 formerly street homeless people. Representatives at each site had the opportunity to review for accuracy our description of their community and its activities for ending chronic street homelessness. Below we present a short introductory sketch of our sites in alphabetical order.

Birmingham, Alabama

Metropolitan Birmingham Services for the Homeless, the entity orchestrating most of the homeless network planning and development that occurs in Birmingham, is a membership organization with no formal authority or control over its members. The network of programs and services developed to encourage people to move from the streets into housing includes outreach, emergency shelter, and transitional and permanent supportive housing. A safe haven[8] is just being developed, with an anticipated opening date of December 2003. Employment and community service are important emphases in programs working with people whose homelessness is complicated by chronic substance abuse. Birmingham has been the site of an ongoing research project funded by the National Institute on Drug Abuse that has had considerable success in treating homeless addicts. Agencies have developed some innovative ways to blend the interests of property owners and poor people to create affordable housing with very little government funding, and have involved the business community in other ways to address street homelessness.

Boston, Massachusetts

Boston has mayoral-level community-wide planning and program development, extensive involvement of mainstream agencies and funding from state and local general revenues, and an extensive and committed community of service providers and advocates working with homeless people. Through a collaborative network of programs and services, the city moves several thousand individuals out of homelessness each year through services such as street outreach and drop-in centers, emergency shelter, substance abuse and mental health treatment, medical services, educational programs, career development and employment services, transportation, and transitional and permanent housing programs. The city has a highly developed approach to discharge planning and homelessness prevention for people with severe mental illness, and is very focused on affordable housing production and preservation.

Columbus, Ohio

The lead agency for the homeless service system in Columbus is the Community Shelter Board (CSB), an independent nonprofit agency founded in 1986 by a group of civic leaders, business associations, local government leaders, and representatives from a variety of foundations. CSB does not provide any direct services within the community, nor is it an original source of money for homeless assistance services. Its main responsibilities are resource development and investment, service delivery coordination and planning, program accountability, and systems change and public policy reform. The Community Shelter Board currently allocates $7.5 million annually to 14 partner agencies for programs serving homeless individuals and families in Columbus.

The community's main strategy for ending chronic homelessness is embodied in an initiative known as "Rebuilding Lives." It is a community-based initiative developed by the Scioto Peninsula Task Force in response to problems created by downtown redevelopment along the part of the riverfront known as the Scioto Peninsula. The task force was charged with developing a coordinated, targeted, cost-effective method of providing shelter and services to homeless individuals and families. Launched in July 1999, the Rebuilding Lives initiative focuses on ending homelessness and "rebuilding lives" by meeting the short-term needs of homeless individuals through an improved safety net of emergency shelters and by establishing 800 units of permanent supportive housing programs for homeless individuals with long-term needs. It includes opportunities for people with severe mental illness, addictions, HIV/AIDS, and combinations to leave the streets for permanent housing with supports in a "housing first" approach that can be as short as three weeks from first contact on the streets to lease signing.

Los Angeles, California

Unlike the other cities we visited, Los Angeles does not offer a single coordinated system for reducing chronic street homelessness, although the Los Angeles Homeless Services Authority (LAHSA) provides funding and guidance for local nonprofit agencies with programs that address homelessness and coordinates the county's Continuum-of-Care applications, in which most of the county's 88 entitlement jurisdictions participate. What Los Angeles does offer, because of its immense size, are several specialized continuums to meet the needs of frequently underserved subgroups of homeless individuals. We visited three such networks that have been working diligently to end chronic street homelessness—the Veterans Affairs Greater Los Angeles Healthcare System (VAGLAHS), Lamp Community, and a state-funded program known as AB 2034 after its legislative bill number. AB 2034 offers integrated services to mentally ill homeless people, and is administered in Los Angeles by the Los Angeles County Department of Mental Health (LAC-DMH). The Department of Veterans Affairs and Lamp Community both offer comprehensive services for homeless individuals, while the AB 2034 program is primarily a funding and coordinating mechanism for service delivery to prevent homelessness upon release for mentally ill offenders in the county jail population. Although these programs do not all work in concert with each other, there is significant overlap among the systems. For example, Lamp Community is a funded program under AB 2034 and at least one VA partner agency collaborates with Lamp Community to provide housing for Lamp guests. Another organization, Shelter Partnership, collaborates with both the AB 2034 program and Lamp Community by providing technical assistance in many areas including housing development, funding, and grant writing. Shelter Partnership also touches many agencies through its advocacy for homeless individuals and its shelter resource bank, which provides surplus merchandise to homeless agencies.

Philadelphia, Pennsylvania

Mayor Wilson Goode in 1988 created the Office of Services for the Homeless and Adults. The office director eventually became a "homeless czar," a position that the next two mayors have maintained and expanded. The current "czar's" official designation is the Deputy Managing Director for Special Needs Housing. Having someone in this position means there is a single person whose obvious job it is to resolve issues about homeless services. This is the Mayor's point person on homeless issues, held responsible for emergency shelter directly but also expected to interact with mainstream systems and coordinate activities more broadly to address homelessness. Through this office and in partnership with a strong array of providers, advocates, and businesses, the city has planned for and subsequently undertaken extensive investment in programs and services to end homelessness.

A major focus of Philadelphia's efforts has been people experiencing chronic street homelessness. The network of programs and services developed to encourage people to move from the streets into housing includes extensive outreach, entry-level safe havens and other low demand residences, emergency shelters, transitional housing programs, permanent supportive housing programs of various configurations, and supportive services purchased or supplied directly by city agencies. These latter services include outreach, mental health and substance abuse treatment and intensive case management, and primary health care. Community development corporations (CDCs), including several created and run by homeless assistance providers, have been active in creating affordable housing that may be occupied by formerly homeless and other persons.

San Diego, California

The Ad Hoc Committee on Downtown Homelessness is San Diego's lead entity for planning and developing resources to end street homelessness in the downtown area. Important differences about San Diego's approach from the community-wide approaches in Philadelphia and Columbus include the informal nature of its lead entity, extensive involvement of the downtown redevelopment agency, Centre City Development Corporation, the Downtown San Diego Partnership, and local law enforcement and the courts in addressing street homelessness, along with the more expected city and county agencies. San Diego's downtown area has undergone redevelopment in recent years, adding a convention center, considerable waterfront development, office buildings, and both market rate and affordable housing. With development of each major downtown section, the homeless street people who frequented the area found themselves displaced. As downtown revitalized, the issue of street homelessness became a focus of discussion. Two police department programs to address street homelessness were already under way when the decision was taken to build a new major league ballpark downtown, in an area that had become the most recent center of street homelessness. The impending ballpark development galvanized San Diego businesses and government agencies to get serious about reducing street homelessness in a responsible way. The network of programs and services developed to encourage people to move from the streets into housing includes outreach, much of which is linked to multi-agency team community policing strategies, emergency shelter, safe havens, and transitional and permanent supportive housing.

Seattle, Washington

Seattle does not have one authority responsible for community-wide strategies to address chronic homelessness. Yet over time, the region has developed an approach to this population as homeless service providers, low-income housing providers, and other agencies involved with chronic street homeless people have cultivated working relationships and capitalized on Federal and local funding opportunities to expand programming. No community-wide coordinating entity controls and manages the full spectrum of resources and services targeting chronic homelessness. Instead, individual nonprofit service providers and government agencies have taken it upon themselves to tackle the problem of chronic street homelessness through specialized service offerings. Some of these agencies work together to meet the needs of their clients while others operate service structures representing the full continuum of care under their own umbrella. Local government leaders—primarily from Seattle and King County—have sponsored various coalitions and task forces over the years that have brought these agencies together to analyze needs, establish priorities, and plan for specific projects and system improvements. Seattle has also responded to Federal funding guidelines concerning programming strategy and initiatives to reduce chronic street homelessness.

Article Organization

We have tried to make this article accessible and practical in several ways. First, we have analyzed the information gathered from the seven communities in cross-cutting chapters that give an overview of a particular topic, including:

- Part 2. Elements of Success
- Part 3. New Strategies for Programs and Services
- Part 4: Assembling Resources and Supports
- Part 5. Documenting Progress
- Part 6. How Communities Pay For Their New Approaches
- Part 7. Policy, Practice, and Research Implications

Second, we present full descriptions of the seven communities we visited and the ways they have approached the job of ending chronic homelessness. These chapters are structured similarly, beginning with a brief community overview followed by a section recapping three to six practices of potential interest to other jurisdictions, including contact information for each practice and a community contact. So readers can go directly to the source to find out more about practices they might want to examine more closely. Each appendix then has sections for the history of the community's approach, a description of that approach, documentation of progress, details of selected system components, funding, maintaining and enhancing the system, and community relations.

Third, the article's final chapter discusses the implications of the findings for policy, practice and research concerning approaches to reducing chronic homelessness.

ELEMENTS OF SUCCESS

What Does It Take?

This chapter introduces the elements that made efforts to reduce chronic street homelessness successful in the study communities. The following chapters elaborate on important aspects of the elements and their interactions, and end with implications for policy, practice, and research. Although we provide examples in the report chapters, the site report appendices provide a more complete description of how the elements of success work together in a specific community.

Introduction

We identified 11 key elements shared by many of the approaches successfully reducing chronic street homelessness. Five of these elements, in combination, are essential for the strongest approaches. In addition to these five elements, trigger events were an important catalytic element for four of our study communities. Five other elements when present contributed to making an approach stronger. The elements were:

Essential Elements
- A paradigm shift;
- A clear goal of ending chronic street homelessness;
- Community-wide level of organization;
- Strong leadership and an effective organizational structure; and
- Significant resources from mainstream public agencies.

Catalyst Element
- Trigger event--capacity to capitalize on triggering events.

Contributing Elements
- Significant resources from the private sector;
- Commitment and support from elected officials;
- Outcome evaluation mechanisms for program support and improvement;
- Openness to new service approaches; and

- Strategies to minimize negative neighborhood reactions to projects.

Paradigm Shift

Of the five essential elements the most important was a paradigm shift away from traditional homeless program goals and approaches. The old paradigm was that street homeless individuals should be cared for more by charitable, often religious, organizations rather than by mainstream public agencies. The old paradigm relied heavily on emergency shelters, transitional housing, and sobriety-based programs. The old paradigm did not plan, or expect, to end chronic street homelessness.

The new paradigm emphasizes reducing and eventually ending chronic street homelessness through an integrated community-wide approach that includes substantial participation by mainstream public agencies. Part of the paradigm shift was the adoption of an explicit goal to end chronic street homelessness. A second part of the shift was communities recognizing that their existing homeless assistance network was not reducing homelessness and that they had to do something different. Permanent supportive housing programs had to expand, they had to be structured to accommodate people with co-occurring disorders, and clear and simple pathways from the street into housing had to be available. The general homeless service programs may remain, but the new programs, supported with new resources, contribute the most to reaching the goal of ending chronic street homelessness.

The paradigm shift to low-demand permanent supportive housing on a broad scale affects policymakers, funders, program planners, and service providers. The new approaches can be especially challenging for traditional housing developers and social service providers. For mental health and social service providers, low-demand environments mean they cannot require tenants to use services, and they have to deal with both mental health and substance abuse issues, and do so simultaneously. In addition, tenants may not use their services consistently, thus reducing reimbursements on which the providers may rely. For housing providers, a low-demand residence means that tenants may not act as predictably as the property managers might wish. For both, the challenges are as much philosophical as financial, in that the new model demands that they conduct business in ways that had formerly been considered not just impractical but wrong (Grieff, Proscio, and Wilkins, 2003).

A Clear Goal of Ending Chronic Street Homelessness

The most successful community-wide approaches have an explicit goal of ending chronic street homelessness. Two communities, Columbus and Philadelphia, have adopted the goal of ending chronic homelessness, which has turned their priorities away from emergency and even transitional programs. They invest heavily in permanent supportive housing and have stabilized (Columbus) or actually reduced (Philadelphia) the number of emergency shelter beds they support as they work to move persistent shelter stayers (Philadelphia) and street homeless people (both cities) into permanent supportive housing. Columbus follows a "housing first" model for chronic street homeless people, moving them directly from the streets into permanent supportive housing, still with low demands. Philadelphia also tries to bypass emergency shelter for street homeless people, but has focused more on safe havens as an intermediate step toward permanent housing and has only recently begun to develop its first "housing first" program.

San Diego has set itself the goal of ending downtown street homelessness, which is a paradigm shift from the city's earlier ways of dealing with street homeless people. It has some unique ways of addressing street homelessness among chronic inebriates and those with severe mental illness and co-occurring disorders, thanks to a police department that has long been in the forefront of community-oriented and problem-solving policing. San Diego developed several safe havens and is working on developing more permanent supportive housing, with active involvement of the local redevelopment authority and the business community.

Strong Community-Wide Level of Organization

A community-wide level of organization exists when agencies are working together to end chronic street homelessness. As we describe organizational approaches, it helps to think about three levels of contact or working together for two or more agencies—communication, coordination, and collaboration (Konrad, 1996; Melaville and Blank, 1991).[9] These levels are hierarchical—agencies cannot coordinate without communicating, and cannot collaborate unless they both communicate and coordinate. The hierarchy reflects the extent to which agencies pay attention to other agencies, perhaps change their own ways, and make a joint effort to reach shared goals. We use these hierarchical terms very carefully throughout this report and define them as follows:

- **Communication.** Agencies are at the level of communication if they have accurate knowledge of each other's existence, service offerings, and eligible clientele. They will also know how to access each other's services, and may refer clients to each other. They may have shared involvements through meetings, committees and task forces, but they do not have mechanisms in place to support each other's work.
- **Coordination.** Agencies are at the level of coordination if in addition to communicating they support each other's efforts to obtain resources for clients. However, they do not deliberately work to develop shared goals and structure their operations to meet these goals.
- **Collaboration.** Agencies are at the level of collaboration if they work with each other to articulate shared goals, analyze their operations to determine how they may achieve those goals, and make the changes dictated by this analysis.

Of course agencies may relate to each other *below* the level of communication—that is, they do not know these things about each other, do not interact in any way, interact negatively, and/or hold inaccurate views of each other. In most communities at most times, most agencies operate toward each other at the level of communication or worse. This is "business as usual"—it takes work to get beyond it.

Collaboration may mean that agency staff members fulfill new roles or restructured roles; co-locate, team, or otherwise work together with staff of other agencies; merge money, issue joint requests for proposals, apply together for new money to do new programs in new ways; actively support each others' work; have mutual feedback mechanisms to assure continued appropriate service and program delivery; and/or other mechanisms and activities that reflect a purposeful, well-thought-out commitment to work together to reach common goals. Collaboration can occur between two agencies, or among several agencies. When it extends to include all or most agencies in a community focused on the same population with the same goals, we call it a strong community-wide level of organization.

Strong Leadership and an Effective Organizational Structure

Strong leadership within an effective organizational structure was crucial in the development of successful community-wide approaches.

The Importance of Key People Exercising Leadership

Ultimately, it is people and not systems that make things happen—especially in the beginning. Individual personality and devotion played an extremely important role in the development of the homeless assistance systems we visited. In most of these communities, a few people have been such essential players that it would be hard to imagine that without them the system would be what it is today. They have not all played the same roles. Some have been idealistic inspirers who brought public and private resources to focus on the issue of chronic street homelessness and stick with it, although their role in the actual organization of services might have been slight. Some have been socially and politically skilled organizational masterminds who knew what it would take to get an aggregation of programs and personalities to become a system focused on chronic street homelessness. Some have occupied vitally important positions in government agencies and persisted over many years in bringing those agencies to the table, keeping them there, and seeing that agency resources were applied to homeless issues, including chronic street homelessness. And some have been instrumental in bringing about a significant meeting of minds because they insist on cooperation and accountability, yet have a high tolerance for tension and the ability to channel it toward useful outcomes. It is vital to recognize the role played by people who really care, and who have the ability to translate that caring into structures of cooperating individuals, programs, and agencies. Without them the homeless assistance systems in their communities would look far different.

We cannot describe the actions and effects of all the leaders in all the communities we visited. However, in the Appendices we describe a few leaders and the effects of their leadership, to show the range of positions in which communities have found leadership, and the capacity of people operating in any position to offer leadership and make a difference.

Effective Organizational Structure

The seven communities we visited for this project have very different structures through which they have developed assistance networks for chronically street homeless people. Most of the communities we visited did not begin their endeavors in the homeless arena with a focus on reducing or ending chronic street homelessness. These focused structures evolved, some over decades, with varying degrees of local political support and local funds. Consequently, they emerged in diverse forms. In Columbus a nonprofit lead agency received strong authority and resources from city, county, business, and philanthropic interests some years before the new initiative. In Philadelphia a combination of a city agency with authority and resources, a Mayor's Task Force, and a voluntary association of all interested parties each play their roles. San Diego developed an informal but well organized group of leaders from relevant positions in the city and county governments and a downtown business association.

What these organizational structures had in common were strong links to elected officials and mainstream governmental and private sector resources. They were not working only in the context of programs for homeless persons. The organizational membership also crossed over city, county, and private sector boundaries. While always coordinating with service providers, the lead organizations did not always include them as full members.

Significant Resources from Mainstream Public Agencies

Ending chronic street homelessness requires resources far beyond those commanded by agencies, programs, and networks exclusively focused on working with homeless people. Major commitments of resources are needed from mainstream public housing, health, mental health, substance abuse, welfare and other agencies.

Mainstream public agencies have four roles to play with respect to ending chronic homelessness. These are facilitating homeless people's access to their services, developing specialty approaches, establishing funding priorities, and contributing leadership of various types.

All of the communities we visited for this study have significant involvement of mainstream public agencies; some have major, sustained commitments and participation in leadership to end chronic homelessness. Most communities in the nation enjoy considerably less mainstream agency involvement, and could benefit from increasing the effectiveness of such partnerships.

Getting mainstream public agencies to the "homeless" table takes planning, persistence, and sometimes power. It also often takes being able to present the case for their involvement as a mutually beneficial situation in which mainstream agencies are able to serve "their own" clients better by joining forces with the local homeless assistance network. The mainstream agencies whose own missions coincide most closely with the goal of ending chronic homelessness, and hence the ones that will have the greatest incentive to work with homeless assistance networks toward that end, include housing and community/neighborhood/economic development agencies; health, mental health, and substance abuse agencies; and to an increasing extent, corrections agencies.

Ability to Capitalize on Trigger Events

In several of the communities we visited, "trigger events" stimulated re-examination of the community's approach to chronic street homelessness. The experiences of these communities in turning trigger events with potentially disastrous consequences for homeless people into opportunities for growth and change provide examples for other communities seeking to develop new approaches to chronic street homelessness.

In two communities the trigger event was proposed development on land that was "home" to many homeless people. In Columbus it was prospective redevelopment of the Scioto Peninsula along Columbus' riverfront; in San Diego it was the prospect of a new downtown ballpark. In two other communities the trigger event was a proposed city ordinance to criminalize street homelessness. One city, Philadelphia, actually passed such an ordinance but not before it had undergone considerable revision and resources had been appropriated to ameliorate its harshest conditions. In the other city, Birmingham, the ordinance was defeated but mobilizing to be sure that happened stimulated some significant forward movement in addressing street homelessness.

Significant Involvement of the Private Sector

In addition to governmental agencies, we found that private businesses and foundations were often mainstream organizations making significant contributions to reducing street homelessness. Their involvement is described more fully in Chapter 4 on assembling resources and supports, but we note a few examples here.

Private Businesses

Many of the communities we visited have been promoting central city redevelopment. In the past many downtown businesses and developers have had a kneejerk reaction against providing services to their neighborhood's street homeless people, fearing that services would attract more homeless individuals. However, in four of our communities, businesses and their associations took leadership roles in programs providing services to help end street homelessness. These were Birmingham, Columbus, Philadelphia, and San Diego.

In the late 1990s the Birmingham City Council was considering an ordinance that would have banned "urban camping," a measure clearly aimed at street homeless people in the downtown area. The proposal galvanized support for an alternative—active outreach programs to bring people off the streets without criminalizing them. Advocates of the ordinance complained that street homeless people were creating problems such as panhandling, litter, poor sanitation, and safety concerns. Advocates for the homeless population wanted to develop a more constructive and less punitive approach. The mayor created a Task Force on Homelessness to address the issue. As an outgrowth of the Task Force, the City Action Partnership (CAP)—the city's Business Improvement District—funded an assistance-oriented uniformed patrol. CAP officers provide services downtown that range from directing shoppers to stores to helping case managers locate homeless individuals when they need to deliver medications or other services. CAP prepares pamphlets listing resources by needs with addresses and maps for food, shelter, clothing, and employment services. CAP officers routinely coordinate with outreach workers from several programs to facilitate assistance to street homeless people.

Columbus businesses play a major role in Community Shelter Board (CSB) fundraising and strategic planning. Business leaders predominate on the CSB's governing board of trustees and have led it to adopt an outcomes-based funding model that has won the respect of agencies and the general public. CSB leverages public grants with corporate fund raising, and private dollars make up over 20 percent of CSB's annual revenue. The private funding helps support innovative programs that have brought Columbus national recognition as a community with creative and effective homeless assistance programs.

Foundations and Nonprofit Organizations

Organizations such as the United Way, which address a wide range of community needs, have the potential to make significant contributions to a community's efforts to end chronic homelessness. In Columbus the United Way helps fund supportive housing for Rebuilding Lives. In Columbus United Way also supports emergency shelter and other CSB initiatives including Rebuilding Lives. The total United Way commitment to the CSB is $1.0 million. In Boston the United Way funded $4 million of emergency shelter, transitional housing, and support services; cash, and in-kind donations from businesses, religious and civic organizations totaled over $3.6 million; and over 50 foundations contributed over $7 million. Cash donations from individuals to programs were also substantial, totaling an additional $12.5 million.

Commitment and Support from Elected Officials

Commitment and support from mayors, city and county councils, and other elected officials can be a significant contributing element in the progress of community-wide efforts toward reducing chronic homelessness. In at least three of our sites, mainstream city officials and business leaders played a seminal role in initiating collaborative programs to end homelessness. Philadelphia's Mayor Goode created an Office of Services for the Homeless and Adults and appointed a de facto "czar" of homeless assistance programs who orchestrated planning and implementing a wide set of services; subsequent mayors maintained and expanded these efforts. Boston's Mayor Menino placed ending homelessness high on his agenda, created a homeless planning committee and pressed mainstream city agencies to become involved. In San Diego mainstream business leaders and city officials involved in mitigating the potential displacement of street homeless persons expected from the construction of a new baseball stadium were among the founders of the interagency Ad Hoc Committee on Downtown Homelessness, which is developing solutions involving housing and services for the special needs homeless population.

State and national political environments also have a significant impact on community approaches to reducing chronic street homelessness. This may be especially true at the state level, which requires a wider mobilization of support than city or county initiatives. Many state assemblies and governors would not follow the examples of California and Massachusetts in making large fiscal commitments to programs to end homelessness. Winning support from elected officials for state and other mainstream funding of programs to end homelessness is greatly facilitated by demonstrations of positive outcomes and cost effectiveness. The potential savings from innovative programs may be demonstrated by developing good estimates of how much homeless persons are costing the public through conventional emergency services and law enforcement programs.

Outcome Evaluation Mechanisms for Program Support and Improvement

Agencies and planners in the communities we visited use data to demonstrate that programs are operating as designed and having successful impacts. The primary types of data we found to document progress in ending chronic street homelessness were:

- Changes in the number of people found on the streets from year to year;
- Increases in the number and percentage of chronically street homeless people who have moved into permanent housing;
- Reductions in costs of providing emergency health, mental health, and shelter services;
- Reductions in days homeless, hospitalized, or incarcerated; and
- Less recidivism in the homeless assistance system, as documented by street counts, program operations and outcome data, and interagency homeless management information system (HMIS) data.

Some street counts were greatly enhanced by asking the homeless individuals background questions. We found examples of communities maintaining information on services provided to individuals in linked emergency shelter and outreach databases, which help in monitoring program activity, evaluating impacts, assessing needs, and planning programs. Some communities also used information systems to demonstrate the incurred costs of providing mainstream emergency services to chronic street homeless individuals—money that could be saved by effective programs to end homelessness. Good administrative record information on homeless-related program operations and outcomes also provide support for program planning, policy design, and system development. In addition, a good homeless management information system can facilitate case management by providing workers access to better case history information and knowledge of what other programs may be serving the client. Finally, some agencies and communities are using analyses based on sound data to support community relations and program advocacy work.

Openness to New Service Approaches

Contributing to the progress of the study communities was their openness to new service approaches. Ending chronic street homelessness requires new approaches to homeless service delivery. It requires new ways of helping people (such as harm reduction), new ways of providing old services (such as housing first), new agency relationships (such as joint provision of mental health and substance abuse services, or agency mergers), and new investments in effective approaches (such as permanent supportive housing). It can also involve redesigning service systems to create better matches between people's needs and the services they receive. One such shift involves reserving emergency shelter and other forms of short-term assistance for those with acute needs who are homeless for the first time or as the result of a crisis, while those with chronic needs receive longer-term supports (including effective treatment for co-occurring mental illness and substance abuse) and permanent housing. (Columbus and Philadelphia are using this strategy.) Reducing chronic street homelessness also results from effective outreach and engagement strategies, especially those that are able to link people directly to housing. Finally, new approaches to prevention can prevent people with chronic disabilities from becoming homeless in the first place.

Strategies to Minimize Negative Neighborhood Reactions to Locating Projects

Frequently, some neighborhood residents resist locating projects for homeless persons in their neighborhood—the "not in my backyard" (NIMBY) reaction. Communities can minimize NIMBY by establishing standards that include looking for favorable locations, planning appropriate structures and activities, and involving the neighborhood in planning. However, the success of these mitigating activities is affected by economic, cultural, and political factors beyond the control of programs. Planning and opening new sites are especially volatile activities that require agencies to establish good communication with neighbors and work to mitigate potential adverse effects. Public meetings with frank descriptions of the project, testimony by neighbors of similar projects, and opportunities for people to express their concerns are essential. (Columbus, Philadelphia, and Seattle employ the strategy of using testimony by people who had seen past projects start up in their neighborhoods.) Forming advisory committees with neighbor representation that address how to resolve problems is also crucial. A good practice is to select locations where rezoning is not necessary and where facilities can be built that improve the neighborhood by removing eyesores and trouble spots. Our sites were able to implement this practice without concentrating their projects in the lowest income areas.

Communities should also have policies that ensure programs are good neighbors once a facility opens. Good neighbor agreements can help promote community relations in the areas of property maintenance, neighborhood codes of conduct, community safety, communication and information, and agreement monitoring and compliance. Agencies can foster better community relations through open houses, making meeting rooms available to neighborhood organizations, participating in neighborhood watch projects and involving the public in fix up and fund raising activities. Staff members can educate neighbors on ways of interacting with homeless individuals and ways of addressing issues they create as a group.

Homeless and formerly homeless individuals can be effective spokespersons to call public attention to their concerns and help develop programs to remedy their problems. These individuals can personalize and associate a human face with the issues by speaking at public meetings.

CONCLUSIONS

This chapter focused on the elements of success separately to provide a clear portrayal of each, however, the combined effects of the elements are what power the greatest community progress toward the goal of ending chronic street homelessness. Of particular importance is the paradigm shift toward a community-wide focus on eliminating chronic street homelessness through mainstream public agency programs including permanent supportive housing.

As we repeatedly stress, this is an experimental time for programs to reduce homelessness, new approaches are being tried and the evaluations of their success are still in emergent stages. Nevertheless, our analyses of the seven study sites, as well as information gathered about other locations during the site selection process, suggest that certain elements are essential for a community to make significant progress toward the goal of ending homelessness. The essential elements were: the paradigm shift; a clear goal of ending chronic street homelessness; community-wide level of organization; strong leadership and an effective organizational structure; and significant resources from mainstream public agencies. At most of our sites, catalytic trigger events combined with a capacity to capitalize on the event led to significant improvements in the community's approach.

We also found the following elements contributed to making a community's approach more effective: significant resources from the private sector; commitment and support from elected officials; outcome evaluation mechanisms for program support and improvement; openness to new service approaches; and strategies to minimize negative neighborhood reactions to projects. Our list of elements emerged and changed over the course of the study, and we do not view it as exhaustive and immutable. It is a snapshot of what we saw happening at this time. The next chapter of the report presents some specific strategies that the communities were incorporating into their approaches for reducing chronic homelessness.

NEW STRATEGIES FOR PROGRAMS AND SERVICES

The number and variety of homeless assistance programs has grown tremendously since the late 1980s and early 1990s, becoming a $2 billion a year endeavor today (National Alliance to End Homelessness, 2000). Yet chronic homelessness remains a serious problem in many communities across the country, despite the system that has been developed to date. As communities come to recognize this reality, they may abandon their old paradigms of what works and shift to new approaches. We described in Chapter 2 how some communities have made this paradigm shift in terms of their general goals and methods. In this chapter we discuss more specifically some successful strategies for reducing chronic homelessness.

Looking at the characteristics of most chronically homeless people, it is obvious that most have serious mental illnesses, substance abuse disorders, HIV/AIDS, or physical disabilities. Many have more than one of these major problems, any one of which frequently results in their being turned away from many traditional homeless assistance programs. Further, they have been homeless a long time, often have no ties to family, and rarely have any resources. Their skills are oriented toward survival on the streets, not to living in housing.

Any effort that expects to reduce chronic homelessness to any significant degree must attract and hold the target population—something that traditional approaches have often failed to do, or the people would not still be homeless. First and foremost, there have to be effective ways to contact and recruit chronically homeless people into programs. Equally important, there must be something to offer them that they will take—the programs need to fit the people, rather than the reverse.

Outreach, housing, and supportive services are obvious components of a solution, but as existing versions of these elements are not doing the job, or not all of the job. New versions have had to be developed. Preventive efforts are also increasingly part of the picture, in the form of planning and providing housing and supports for people at high risk of homelessness on being discharged from institutions. More and more communities have recognized that their outreach, housing, supportive services, and discharge planning must incorporate the following abilities if they are going to be part of the solution to chronic homelessness:

The ability to attract people with addictions. Many chronically homeless people are initially unwilling to commit to sobriety. If programs cannot work with people who are still using alcohol and drugs, they cannot attract the hard-core street homeless people.

The ability to attract people with serious mental illnesses. Many chronically homeless people have serious mental illnesses that have affected their willingness to use shelters. They often find shelters intolerable because of overcrowding, or feel vulnerable and threatened by fellow residents, or the shelters themselves will not serve them because their symptoms are too disruptive.

The willingness and ability to accept and work with people with co-occurring disorders. Too many chronically homeless people have been caught in the demands of single-focus agencies, within both homeless-specific and mainstream systems. Many agencies will not work with people's mental illness until they stop using substances, or will not work with their substance abuse until their psychiatric symptoms are under control.

At the same time communities have been seeing the advantages of interagency databases, multi-agency teams, multi-purpose service centers, and processes to increase access to mainstream agencies. In this chapter, we examine the ways that programs and services can reduce chronic homelessness by accommodating to the needs of the people they want to reach.

Outreach

Outreach and engagement are the first steps involved in connecting with street homeless people, bringing them off the streets, and linking them with other portions of the service system. Most chronically homeless people are unlikely to connect with even the best housing programs unless these first contacts are effective. Our study communities provide several examples of new strategies to make outreach more effective.

Philadelphia's Outreach Coordination Center

Philadelphia's Outreach Coordination Center (OCC) developed in 1998 as part of the city's commitment to develop systematic approaches to ending street homelessness following enactment of a Sidewalk Behavior Ordinance. Its innovative aspects include outreach teams from several agencies working together and coordinated through a single entity, the OCC; daytime rather than nighttime outreach; direct access to safe havens and other low demand residences that were developed simultaneously; full cooperation and backup from city health, mental health, and substance abuse agencies; and a comprehensive database. The OCC also operates in an environment with existing and increasing permanent supportive housing resources.

The OCC offers a coordinated point of contact for street homeless people. Outreach workers linked to the OCC are able to offer a wide array of services. Even more important, at a meeting of 17 outreach workers, all said they felt confident that the people they contact will receive the services if they are willing to accept them. One does not always find such confidence among outreach workers in other cities, as the services often are not sufficient to meet demand, or not geared to street homeless people.

The OCC coordinates most of the city's outreach efforts, including a 24-hour homeless hotline, one comprehensive response team, two mental health specialty teams, two substance abuse specialty teams (one peer and one professional), and emergency backup from city agencies. The teams cover center city and west and southwest Philadelphia, where the majority of chronically homeless individuals who avoid shelters are found. In addition to these regular street "beats," OCC outreach workers respond to hotline calls from businesses, civic and neighborhood associations, and private citizens about homeless people in need. OCC has a case management component and access to the city's list of available shelter beds. Representatives of all outreach teams meet monthly to review activities and needs. Through radio contact with teams, the OCC facilitates resolution of the immediate needs of any homeless person in contact with an outreach worker on the street that the worker cannot handle independently. OCC workers have also conducted street counts of homeless people every quarter since 1998, and are now doing it monthly.

Since its inception, OCC has maintained a database of all persons contacted by the participating outreach teams, averaging about 2,000 unduplicated individuals annually. OCC teams repeatedly see about one-fourth of those they contact over a span of years. These are the chronic street homeless people the teams try hardest to induce off the streets. The database provides a history of their service receipt and an excellent picture of who they are and what their needs are. Through common identifiers, the OCC database can be linked with the city's database that chronicles most emergency shelter and some transitional housing stays. Using this link, OCC workers can see whether any of their consumers have used shelter, and how much. Conversely, the city's analysts can assess the proportion of people making heavy use of emergency shelter who are also well known to outreach workers.

San Diego's Police-Based Outreach Teams

San Diego city has two innovative outreach programs developed by and located in the San Diego Police Department—the Homeless Outreach Team (HOT) and the Serial Inebriate Program (SIP). Both can offer housing options that bypass emergency shelter, connecting street homeless people directly to safe havens, transitional housing programs, or residential treatment settings.

HOT combines a police officer, a mental health worker, and a benefits eligibility technician in outreach teams operating during the day and evening hours to engage mentally ill street people and connect them to services. It also has access to "dedicated" safe haven beds to which it can bring people if they are willing to leave the streets. The team approaches people on the street or at homeless services. Each HOT team member's skills and agency affiliation enhances those of the others, to make the combination more effective than any one or two acting without the others. Because they combine police and mental health expertise and authority, they are the only outreach teams on the streets that have the ability to remove people either voluntarily or involuntarily, in addition to building rapport and making referrals. The mental health worker opens up options for care that the police officer could not access, the police officer adds an element of protection and authority that the mental health worker could not command, and the eligibility technician offers connection to or reinstatement of benefits that serves as a positive inducement for street people to accept services. HOT focuses on people who are likely to have mental illness as a primary problem and are not likely to get arrested. HOT gets them into treatment facilities, safe havens, board and care facilities, and skilled nursing facilities, depending on their level and type of need. When HOT encounters alcoholics or other substance abusers it offers rehabilitation and help getting into appropriate care for those who are interested.

SIP comes into play for chronic inebriates who do not voluntarily accept treatment. SIP is a collaboration of four city and five county agencies, including law enforcement, the city attorney's office, the public defender, the Superior Court, health care, and homeless agencies working as a team in a court context. Mental Health System, Inc. is contracted to coordinate the program. SIP follows the Drug Court model in offering addicts a choice of jail or treatment, after assuring that the community was willing to pay for treatment if requested. SIP's focus is on chronic alcoholics who populate the downtown streets of San Diego. Police officers arrest chronic street alcoholics for public drunkenness, and bring them to jail and subsequently to court. Once arraigned, caseworkers approach each person, conduct assessments, and offer treatment plus transitional housing as an alternative to six months in jail (the maximum allowed under California state law) to those who pass the assessment. Many people eventually accept the offer, although they may first serve a full jail sentence or even two before they are convinced to try. The court monitors treatment compliance; leaving treatment means returning to jail. This approach is "something different" for this population, for which the revolving door of arrest and detoxification was not working. The approach is also designed to reduce the impact of public drunkenness on the community.

Other Outreach Efforts with Direct Housing Connections

In Los Angeles we also found innovative outreach efforts focused on well-defined subpopulations of chronically homeless people—veterans, and mentally ill criminal offenders. Both efforts were part of larger programs that included housing and supportive services as well as health, mental health, and other types of care. Their involvement in a collaborative network of public and private agencies and their connection to housing should make them interesting to other communities.

The Veterans Affairs Greater Los Angeles Healthcare System has used Health Care for Homeless Veterans programs to conduct outreach to severely mentally ill veterans to link them with VA clinical services, contracted residential treatment programs, and contracted transitional or permanent supported housing programs. The VA operates some of these programs on its own campus, and has developed an elaborate system of contracts with nonprofit agencies to supply a variety of housing and service options. Also in Los Angeles, the County Sheriff's and Mental Health Departments and nonprofit mental health providers collaborate in a partially state-funded program to prevent first or repeat homelessness among inmates of the county jail who have a serious mental illness. The program begins with integrated outreach focused on individuals who are homeless, at risk of homelessness or incarceration, and who have a serious mental illness.

In Seattle, the Downtown Emergency Service Center (DESC) operates many programs and services that make it a mini-continuum in its own right, all focused on street homeless people. One of its programs is outreach, which is able to connect street homeless people to the various DESC offerings including transitional and permanent supportive housing. DESC's Homeless, Outreach, Stabilization, and Transition Project (HOST) has Outreach and Engagement Specialists who work within specific geographic regions or in other targeted programs or facilities such as drop-in centers for women, local hospitals, and jails to find chronically street homeless people and help them connect to services and housing. Sometimes they approach potential clients directly and other times they develop an engagement plan with staff members from other agencies who have had interactions with the person. HOST staff members receive referrals from concerned citizens, jail, the Department of Social and Health Services, the mental health court, hospitals, the Harborview Medical Center Crisis Triage Unit, the Seattle Public Library, family members, and other mental health professionals, shelters, and drop-in centers.

Other Outreach Efforts without Direct Housing Connections

Every community we visited has outreach and engagement programs that are less fortunate than those already mentioned, in that they have no direct access to housing options for the street people they contact. However successful the outreach to people living on the streets, its value is limited in terms of ending chronic street homelessness if the community does not have adequate permanent supportive housing or safe haven resources. Large congregate emergency shelters are unlikely to succeed in breaking the cycle of chronic street homelessness among people with multiple disabilities. Traditional shelters also tend to be places where chronically homeless street people are not willing to go and stay for extended periods of time. During a focus group discussion of formerly chronically homeless men who were housed in various PSH programs, the group was asked what they would do in the absence of the program. Interestingly, several commented that they would never want to go back to a shelter—they were more willing to return to the streets than to a shelter.

Nevertheless, many outreach programs are able to help street homeless people in a variety of ways even when they are not able to offer them a home. In addition to providing a regular contact and a reliable friend on the street, they are able to ease the difficulties of street living. We describe one such program here, of several we encountered during site visits—Seattle's Mental Health Chaplaincy.

The Mental Health Chaplaincy provides an outreach and engagement program for the most difficult and most vulnerable mentally ill street homeless people. Its outreach strategy involves long-term engagement with clients until they receive benefits and are comfortable entering into service or housing programs. The Chaplaincy program helped to develop and uses the Relational Outreach and Engagement Model currently promulgated by the National Health Care for the Homeless Council.[10] This model has four phases to working with homeless individuals: approach, companionship, partnership, and mutuality, which revolve around building and shaping a relationship with the client. The focus is to build trust with street people until they are ready to access services on their own terms. The Mental Health Chaplaincy typically will link its clients to other Seattle service providers such as Harborview Mental Health, local emergency rooms, the Downtown Emergency Service Center, and the Health Care for the Homeless Network.

New Approaches to Permanent Supportive Housing

The ultimate solution for ending homelessness of any type is housing. For chronically homeless people with disabilities, though, simple housing is not enough. Most people who have been living on the streets for many years have multiple barriers to independent living and are likely to need various treatment and support services for many years. A major innovative step in reducing chronic homelessness among people with disabilities was taken in the early 1990s (and even earlier in some places such as Philadelphia), when models of permanent housing with attached supportive services were developed. Demonstration studies sponsored by NIMH (Shern et al., 1997) showed that permanent supportive housing (PSH) was very successful at stabilizing its tenants in housing, with retention rates at about 85 percent after two years or more. As PSH programs evolved, they embodied most or all of a set of principles since articulated by the Technical Assistance Collaborative as:[11]

- The housing is affordable for people with SSI level incomes (residents usually pay 30 percent of income or about $160 per month);
- There is choice and control over living environment;
- The housing must be permanent (tenant/landlord laws apply, but refusal to participate in services is not grounds for eviction);
- The housing is "unbundled" from but linked to services;
- The supports are flexible and individualized: not defined by a "program"; and
- There is integration of services, personal control, accessibility, and autonomy.

Although it is not a principle, in the past a characteristic of many PSH programs has been that prospective tenants had to be "housing ready." This almost always meant "clean and sober," stabilized on medications if mental illness was an issue, and familiar with the rudiments of housekeeping. As a consequence, very few people entered these programs directly from the streets. The usual routes could be long, through emergency shelter and transitional housing programs. Another consequence is that as of 2002, a surprisingly small proportion of PSH units appear to be occupied by people that we would consider to have been chronically homeless—only about 20 percent, according to a recent Corporation for Supportive Housing estimate.[12]

Thus, although some chronically homeless disabled people are being served in the PSH programs developed during the past decade, the people on whom this project focuses are, by definition, those for whom traditional programs and services have not produced solutions to homelessness. One group in particular, people with co-occurring mental illness and substance abuse, has traditionally been seen as "resistant to treatment." They have been beyond the reach of many traditional homeless service providers, in part because they are "difficult" but also in part because providers have not been interested in trying to serve them, having enough easier people to serve. But as they comprise a significant share of street homeless people, communities committed to reducing street homelessness had to find ways to serve them. Their resistance even to PSH as it was being offered, and also the resistance of many providers to serving them, has challenged communities to develop permanent supportive housing operating on some new, or additional, principles. In the communities we visited, these include:

- Housing first models that place people directly from the streets into permanent housing units with appropriate supportive services;
- Safe havens, a variation of Housing First that offers "as long as you need it" accommodation but that nevertheless is not intended to be permanent;
- Low demand—breaking the linkage between housing and service use or acceptance; and
- Harm reduction or "abstinence encouraged" approaches to sobriety.

Housing First Models

Housing First models place people directly from the streets into permanent housing units with appropriate supportive services, with no requirement that they be "housing ready." The sole requirements are those that are usually expected of any renter—pay the rent, do not destroy the property, and refrain from violence. Housing is provided immediately, with few, if any, demands with respect to abstinence or accepting mental health treatment or other types of care, although these are offered and available. As one advocate for PSH and Housing First puts it, "we give them a key to their own door; they don't have to leave it open, but we knock often." Proponents of this approach argue that it is much easier to work on substance abuse and mental health issues when clients are stably housed than when they are on the streets or in a shelter. More and more communities are attempting to offer chronically homeless street people Housing First. Among the communities we visited, Columbus, San Diego, Seattle, and two of the Los Angeles sites offer Housing First programs, and Philadelphia is just starting to do so. Also, a growing body of research documents the success of Housing First models at keeping even the most disabled homeless people housed, and also saves some public costs for crisis emergency services (Anderson et al; 2000; Culhane, Metraux and Hadley, 2002; Martinez and Burt, 2003; Tsemberis and Eisenberg, 2000).

Housing First programs are very popular among outreach workers, case managers, and their clients. Those we interviewed as part of this study reported that they could easily fill their permanent supportive housing programs with chronic street homeless people, and the tenants in such programs are very positive about them. Of course, slots in permanent housing programs are not always available. In Columbus, Ohio, recruitment for these programs tends to happen when a program first opens for occupancy. Turnover among tenants has been much lower than expected, so the most common way in is at start-up. Also in San Diego, efforts to recruit chronically homeless people directly from the streets into PSH (or safe havens when no PSH unit is immediately available) are ongoing and successful.

Safe Havens

"Safe haven" is a term used by HUD and others to describe a special type of housing program for chronically homeless people with serious mental illness, often with co-occurring substance abuse. A safe haven program usually takes a Housing First approach, and it may be either transitional or permanent housing. Most safe haven programs we talked with will let residents stay "as long as it takes" for them to feel comfortable moving on. Data from Philadelphia's four safe havens indicate that the average length of stay is 1.3 years, and that most residents move on to PSH or to housing in the community, either independently or with family. Three of the communities we visited, Philadelphia, San Diego, and Seattle, have safe havens, and Birmingham will open one in December 2003. In both Philadelphia and San Diego, capacity and turnover appear to be such that a safe haven bed is usually available when a street homeless person is ready and willing to take it. Seattle's safe haven is usually full, however, and not able to accommodate the many more people on the streets who could and would use this type of program.

Low Demand—Breaking the Linkage between Housing and Service Acceptance

A key component of Housing First and safe haven models is their willingness to accept tenants without requiring that they participate in services. As already mentioned, the only demand placed on tenants in these programs is that they adhere to the conditions of their lease (Housing First), or the equivalent without a lease (safe haven). An example of a restrictive condition that remains is that projects funded by HUD bar the use of illegal drugs on the premises. Another restriction is that some projects require clients to participate in a representative payee program for the purpose of assuring that the rent is paid. In many ways, the low demand concept entails significant changes that affect policymakers, funders, program planners, and service providers. The new approaches can be especially challenging for traditional housing developers and social service providers. For mental health and social service providers, low demand environments mean that a tenant does not have to use services, or use them consistently. Providers have to *attract* tenants to services, so the services, and the providers, have to be attractive *to the very resistant people* they are trying to serve. In addition, service providers may not be able to count on a predictable level of reimbursements for services, upon which their budgets may depend. For housing providers, low demand programs may mean that tenants may not always act as predictably as property managers might wish, and that housing managers may have to deal directly with tenants rather than going through service providers. For both, the challenges are as much philosophical as financial, because low demand housing sometimes means that they must now conduct business in ways that had formerly been considered not just impractical but wrong.[13] Much of the debate surrounding Housing First and safe haven models concerns how substance abuse and mental health issues are handled, to which we now turn.

New Approaches to Addressing Substance Abuse

A central tenet of low demand housing is not requiring sobriety. These sobriety "preferred but not required" conditions often translate into a "no use on the premises" rule for projects that use HUD funds. The terms "low" or "no" demand housing describe programs where abstinence may be encouraged but is not required or enforced. This is one aspect of a more general movement known as "harm reduction" within the broader health treatment community of which programs for disabled homeless people are a part.

Harm Reduction

Harm reduction may guide the operations of either permanent or transitional supportive housing. Harm reduction is a set of practical strategies designed to reduce the negative consequences of drug use by promoting first safer use, then managed use, and finally abstinence if people can do it.[14]

In their position statement on housing options for individuals with serious mental illness, the American Association of Community Psychiatrists advocates a full range of community-based housing types, including the following:

- **"Abstinence-expected ("dry") housing**: This model is most appropriate for individuals with substance disorders who choose abstinence, and who want to live in a sober group setting to support their achievement of abstinence. Such models may range from typical staffed group homes to supported independent group sober living. In all these settings, any substance use is a program violation, but consequences are usually focused and temporary, rather than "one strike and you're out."

- **Abstinence-encouraged ("damp") housing**: This model is most appropriate for individuals who recognize their need to limit use and are willing to live in a supported setting where uncontrolled use by themselves and others is actively discouraged. However, they are not ready or willing to be abstinent. Interventions focus on dangerous behavior, rather than substance use per se. Motivational enhancement interventions are usually built into program design.

- **Consumer-choice ("wet") housing**: This model has had demonstrated effectiveness in preventing homelessness among individuals with persistent homeless status and serious psychiatric disability (Tsemberis and Eisenberg, 2000). The usual approach is to provide independent supported housing with case management (or ACT) wrap-around services, focused on housing retention. The consumer can use substances as he chooses (though recommended otherwise) except to the extent that use-related behavior specifically interferes with housing retention. Pre-motivational and motivational interventions are incorporated into the overall treatment approach."[15]

Not surprisingly, the last two options are controversial, and projects that use HUD funds cannot permit illegal drug use on the premises. Nevertheless, for people with long-term deeply rooted problems, these options appear to be among the ones that work best, in part because they are the ones that this group of people is willing to try, and in part because the approach to services is one they can live with. Participants in focus groups for this project repeatedly stressed the importance of having control over their own service uptake, and that staff respect their right to move at their own pace. Harm reduction programs have been the last type of PSH to appear in many communities, and in many areas programs using this approach are not available at all. Yet it has great potential for preventing and ending homelessness, especially among people who have "failed" sober group living.

The fundamental belief underlying Housing First and most other low demand housing strategies is that individuals should not be left homeless simply because they are unable or unwilling to maintain abstinence. Among the communities we visited, Columbus and Seattle have extensive harm reduction-based programs, Lamp in Los Angeles was an early Housing First and harm reduction developer, Philadelphia's safe havens and many of its

PSH programs operate on a harm reduction model, as will the Housing First program it is getting ready to open, and San Diego has similar housing opportunities.

Other Approaches

In addition to harm reduction programs, we observed a number of other innovative intervention strategies for homeless chronic substance abusers during our site visits for this project. Two are expansions and enhancements of traditional detoxification programs, while a third combines community service and employment expectations with traditional clean and sober requirements. A fourth approach, San Diego's Serial Inebriate Program, has already been described in the Outreach section of this chapter.

The two examples of expanding traditional detoxification programs are Maryhaven Engagement Center in Columbus, Ohio and the Dutch Shisler Sobering Center in Seattle. People may walk into these programs on their own, or be brought by outreach workers or law enforcement officials. Once there, they are strongly encouraged to stay and sober up and then to move on to longer residential treatment programs. These communities have made an effort to develop extended residential treatment, recognizing that without it detox is usually just a revolving door.

Several programs for homeless chronic substance abusers in Birmingham take a very different tack. They require sobriety, community service, and employment, as well as attendance at regular meetings related to staying clean. Community service begins immediately, at a level of 10-20 hours a week, and clearly functions as much more than a way to keep participants occupied. In a large focus group held in Birmingham with people who had been chronically homeless, most said that being required to perform community service was the first time in their lives that anyone had treated them as if they had something to contribute, and as if they had a community that would care what they gave. This was the turning point and beginning of self-esteem for most people at the focus group. Community service continues even after employment begins, which occurs as soon as a person's sobriety indicates it is feasible. Programs have developed extensive networks of employers willing to hire program participants, and several programs said finding work for people was not a problem. Working continues the self-esteem boost begun by community service, and puts people on the road to self-sufficiency. Program graduates often help locate jobs, and some have become employers themselves, as well as organizers of community service opportunities. Noting that participants frequently could not sustain sobriety after residential treatment if they went back into the community, several Birmingham substance abuse programs developed transitional housing and affordable private housing. One has become the biggest affordable housing developer in the area, serving formerly homeless and never homeless low-income people alike. In Birmingham, PSH is reserved largely for those with serious mental illness, with or without co-occurring disorders, and people with AIDS. Chronic substance abusers are expected to work from very early in their recovery, to contribute to the cost of their program (they pay for both emergency shelter and transitional housing as soon as they are working), and ultimately to become self-sufficient.

Housing Configurations and Supportive Services

PSH housing configurations vary a great deal, which in turn affects decisions about how to offer supportive services and whether it is also possible to create a supportive community of tenants. Completely scattered-site configurations (program participants occupy apartments wherever they can find them, usually no more than one or two in any single building) make demands on service delivery that are quite different from the opportunities offered by operating a dedicated building (one in which all tenants are part of the program). Other housing configurations include "clustered scattered" and mixed-use buildings. "Clustered" programs may operate a six- or eight-unit building completely occupied by program participants on a block with no other such buildings. Mixed-use buildings are usually large (100-300 units), with 20 to 25 percent of units set aside for program tenants. Other tenants may be never-homeless disabled singles, as is the case at Sunshine Terrace in Columbus, a public housing authority 811 building.[16] Or they may be "regular" low-income households, as in the unit set-asides in the San Diego buildings developed by Centre City Redevelopment Authority. Set-aside units may be master-leased by a PSH program or accessed through an understanding with landlords that on average, every fourth vacant unit will go to a program client. Another variation on "mixed" use is a building occupied entirely by formerly homeless people, in which tenants may include both singles and families.

Support services in these programs may include case management, service referrals, instruction in basic life skills, alcohol/drug abuse treatment, mental health treatment, health care (medical, dental, vision, and pharmaceutical), AIDS-related treatments, income support, education, employment and training assistance, communication services (telephone, voice mail, e-mail, Internet access), transportation, clothing, child care, and legal services. The exact mix of services and who provides them can vary greatly from one community to another, and even from one program to another in the same community. This variation is partly a result of who does what in different communities, and partly due to the "piece-it-together-as-best-you-can" nature of assembling the many types of people, agencies, and funding streams needed to create a successful supportive housing program. However, the variety is also partly deliberate, as programs and communities sort out the most effective distribution of responsibilities among housing developers, property managers, on-site program service staff, and services delivered on and off site by staff of other agencies. And it is always influenced by housing configurations.

Issues mentioned during our site visits that affect supportive services structure include:

- **The appropriate division of labor between property management and case management.** Most programs we visited have decided to separate these two functions, either by assigning them to completely different entities (such as a housing management company for the first and the program for the second) or by dividing their own staff into distinct property management and services teams. This eliminates the conflict of interest that arises in handling nonpaying tenants or other issues relating to lease conditions.

- **Whether to bring services into the residential site or encourage tenants to navigate community service systems.** This is not a major issue in scattered-site programs, but it is in mixed-use and dedicated buildings. Program staff members say tenants often prefer that services come to them. As they use services more when the services are convenient, staff members have some motivation to accommodate the tenants. This is especially true as these are PSH programs where tenants are not expected to be working toward self-sufficiency, and the demand that they deal directly with service systems may be enough to prevent them from getting the services they need.

- **The extension of services to tenants of mixed-use buildings who are not part of the program, and who were never homeless.** Several communities (Columbus, at Sunshine Terrace; Seattle, through Plymouth Housing) have found this to be both useful and cost-effective.

- **How to attract tenants to services when they are free to choose to use them or not.** Housing First and safe haven programs need to make effective *offers* of service, as they cannot require tenants to use services. Program staff in many of the communities we visited characterized their role as making friends, being available, making suggestions, checking up, hanging out, creating and then attending social events such as barbeques or monthly birthday parties, either not having an office or never closing the door, and other similar measures. Tenant word-of-mouth is the best referral; acting in ways contrary to tenant free choice will quickly be known and compromise one's ability to assist tenants. For many service professionals, this is really a whole new way of life.
- **How much the on-site program staff should know about what services tenants are accessing.** Some programs arrange for sensitive issues such as mental health and substance abuse to be handled by contract service providers who offer their services on site but independent of the program staff. Tenants make their own arrangements to see these service providers, and information of what they wanted and what they got is never conveyed to the program staff. Strict confidentiality is maintained. Other programs handle these issues with program staff, still maintaining strict confidentiality and voluntary use of services.
- **How to maximize service dollars, which may also be related to facilitating tenant access to services**. To facilitate client access, many homeless assistance programs use program staff, supported by grant monies, to provide health, mental health, substance abuse, as well as case management. Medicaid might be able to cover these services, freeing up grant monies, but the programs are not set up to maintain the records Medicaid requires, to do Medicaid billing, or to underwrite costs during what may be long lag times before reimbursement occurs. San Diego addresses many of these issues simultaneously through contracts with nonprofit and for-profit behavioral health companies—see Chapter 6 for a description.

Preventing Homelessness Upon Institutional Discharge

One of the most effective ways of ending chronic street homelessness is preventing it from happening in the first place. This often involves commitment of resources to assure housing and services, and effective discharge planning from the many institutions that interface with chronically homeless people and those at risk of chromic homelessness: hospitals, treatment facilities, psychiatric institutions, correctional facilities, and sometimes foster care. In the absence of effective policies and practices around discharge, many of these institutions simply release people into local homeless shelters. Even discharge planning without commitment of resources to assure stable housing, is not sufficient to prevent homelessness. Discharge plans adequate to prevent homelessness typically include an estimated discharge date, collecting medical records, and making arrangements for post-release housing, medical and mental health care, and other community-based services. In some states this planning is the formal responsibility of the agency releasing the individual back into the community, while in other places it is done more informally by agency staff or community-based social service providers (Community Shelter Board, 2002). Our study discovered many examples of important prevention efforts, but did not focus strongly on them because we knew that HUD has two other studies focused specifically on prevention. One is on discharge planning to prevent street homelessness among ex-offenders, and the other is a more general look at the workings of successful community programs to prevent homelessness of all types.

Philadelphia's Housing Support Center (HSC). The HSC has a primary prevention focus for individuals (and families) at imminent risk of homelessness. It began operations in winter 2003, and when fully operational will bring together resources from Adult Services, Department of Human Services (child welfare), Community Behavioral Health, the County Assistance Office (cash assistance), the Philadelphia Housing Authority, and other public agencies whose clients face challenges to housing stability. It will serve as the city's central referral point for all households needing help because they are facing or experiencing homelessness. Because Philadelphia has a homeless management information system that covers all emergency shelter and another that covers the street population, the city will be able to track whether people assisted by the HSC do indeed avoid becoming homeless.

Psychiatric Institution Discharge Planning. A number of communities, including Boston and Columbus, have policies and structures in place to prevent people leaving public psychiatric facilities from becoming homeless.

Correctional Institutions Discharge Planning. Boston and Los Angeles (County Sheriff's Department), and at least some other California cities have programs to prevent homelessness among mentally ill offenders leaving correctional institutions. The Los Angeles program, funded through California state revenues in the AB 2034 program, involves careful interagency coordination as part of making discharge planning work. The Program Evaluator links the client with an agency in the area where he wishes to reside after discharge. If no housing is available in the client's desired area, he is placed close by and has the option of receiving outpatient treatment in the program of his choice until housing becomes available. Once in the program, the individual may transfer between programs as the need arises. Even though the jail does not have a policy requiring housing upon release, the agencies participating in the AB 2034 program are required to locate housing and provide transportation to wherever the client will be living upon release. Checks are in place to assure that incarcerated AB 2034 clients are not discharged to the streets.

Leaving Substance Abuse Treatment. In some communities, individual agencies such as the Community Psychiatric Clinic in Seattle and Aletheia House in Birmingham have created a continuum of housing options, starting with residential treatment and including transitional, permanent supportive, and affordable independent housing, because they perceived that many such clients became homeless without these options. Both programs serve people who have never been homeless as well as those who have. They offer primary prevention to the former, and secondary prevention to the latter.

Client-Level Coordination Mechanisms

In addition to strategies involving new types of programs and new treatment philosophies, we encountered quite a number of mechanisms for assuring that individual clients get the services they need. These client-level service coordination mechanisms are the grease that makes the wheels go round for the new strategies and philosophies. Without them, clients would not have the same chance of getting the services they need, especially when they have many and complex needs that require assistance from many types of agencies. These client-level coordinating mechanisms include databases, various multi-agency team and co-location mechanisms.

Databases
One way that community agencies can promote appropriate service delivery to individual clients is to share information about the services that each provides. A number of communities use database technology to do just

that. Some communities have created databases specifically for the homeless population and services while others use existing databases to track their clients' use of mainstream services or systems. Using databases allows staff members of one agency to know what services someone might be receiving from others, and plan their own service delivery accordingly. Shared databases also help agencies avoid unnecessary service duplication. Databases are useful at each level of community interaction and can be forms of communication, coordination, or collaboration, depending on how agencies related to each other overall.

King County's Mental Health Information System is a database used for both communication and coordination purposes. King County's Mental Health System has a Mental Health Information System logging any person's use of county mental health services. This database has become a source of useful information for Seattle's homeless service providers that are also certified mental health providers such as the Downtown Emergency Service Center. Individuals who have used system services have a record in the shared database and get a rating, or tier, for their service needs. To enroll a new client, he or she must first be on or eligible for Medicaid. Then the agency serving the client will apply for a tier based on medical necessity and treatment intensity. The county will review the tier request and grant or deny the tier. Once tiered, the person can begin to receive ongoing publicly funded treatment.

The Mental Health Information System serves a communication function related to service duplication. The database logs the person's tier and the agency that provides care within the mental health system; two agencies cannot serve the same individual and both receive reimbursement for the care. The database thus prevents mental health service duplication and encourages some interaction among agencies to provide the most appropriate services. For example, if an outreach worker begins to provide outreach and engagement services to a street homeless individual who already gets services from another agency, the worker will reconnect the person to the original agency to continue services. Or if the person seems to need the specific services of the agency doing outreach, the staff will contact the other agency and ask them to stop providing services to the individual so they can begin to.

The Mental Health Information System also serves a coordinating function in Seattle between mental health service providers and local hospitals and jails. Once a person is logged in the database, a countywide agreement assures that local jails and hospitals notify the mental health provider if its client becomes incarcerated or is admitted for services. Then the mental health provider is encouraged to contact the client to re-establish or refine service linkages.

Other communities use database technology as part of their collaborative work. The San Diego REACH Project (Reaching Out and Engaging to Achieve Consumer Health) makes use of an existing database to assist its clients. This program, operating under the aegis of the San Diego County Mental Health Services Department, contracts with the San Diego County Probation Department to have a probation officer assigned to work directly with the REACH team. The officer is able to access the Department of Corrections database and helps many REACH clients clear up outstanding legal issues (e.g., warrants, criminal background checks) in her role as liaison between clients and the courts.

The Greater Los Angeles Department of Veteran Affairs (VAGLAHS) created a database to assist with its work with agencies in its collaborative network. Staff members developed a discharge/service history database that provides the ability to track the service-use patterns of individual veterans. The discharge/service history database logs individuals' use of services throughout the whole homeless services network. VAGLAHS program and partner agency staff members contact the VAGLAHS database coordinator to provide client data and the database coordinator also periodically contacts partner agencies to ensure that all data have been submitted. Partner agencies also contact the database coordinator to learn about a new enrollee's history of service receipt and use the information to develop an appropriate service approach. VAGLAHS staff liaisons to partner agencies also use this database to review veteran status and to ensure appropriate referral and service plans.

Philadelphia's OCC, which was discussed above in this chapter's section on outreach, is a particularly strong example of a collaborative service network using an integrated database. The agencies collaborate to integrate outreach efforts so that different teams cover different areas of the city and/or different issues of immediate concern. The collaborative has created a database to log the outreach and case management contacts. Outreach workers can also access shelter and transitional housing information by linking into the database maintained by the city that tracks this information.

Multi-Agency Special Case Teams

In addition to the multi-agency teams that collaborate on a day-to-day basis, such as those discussed in this chapter's outreach section, there are teams that collaborate on a case-by-case basis or for a particular subset of the client population. Multi-agency special case teams may work for agencies that recognize the utility of combining approaches and integrating services, but may not have the resources to address the needs of all clients so they focus on cases meeting particular criteria.

An example of a multi-agency special case team is Seattle's High Users of Crisis Public Services team. Every two weeks staff members from the Crisis Triage Unit in the Harborview Medical Center Emergency Room, the REACH project (an outreach and case management project for chronic public inebriates), the emergency room, the Sobering Center, the detoxification center, the Emergency Service Patrol (a transport system for chronic public inebriates) and other relevant service providers meet to discuss high service users. These are people who have used the Crisis Triage Unit four times in three months, of which 52 percent are homeless. Together the agencies create integrated service plans for clients that each provider commits to following. This system allows service providers to think together creatively about client needs and the types of services that would be helpful to particular individuals, focusing especially on services designed to reduce their reliance on expensive public services. Clients sign information releases so agencies can coordinate in this way. At times the Triage Unit may also involve the client, family, friends, or police representatives.

In Los Angeles, the VAGLAHS collaborative network is another example of a multi-agency special case team. The VA has an administrative requirement that a homeless veteran is only eligible for three complete treatment episodes in residential programs. If a person requires more than three episodes in housing, then the VA is required to seek a waiver for the person. The network uses the discharge/service history database just described to see whether a person has reached his service limit. When that happens, staff members from the VAGLAHS and relevant collaborating programs, as well as the veteran, come together in a clinical case conference to develop an approach to care to meet the person's needs at that point. The group develops a service plan and integrated service approach that the participating agencies commit to following. If necessary, the VAGLAHS staff will apply for a waiver for a client.

Multi-Purpose Service Centers

Another way that agencies collaborate around services for chronically homeless people is to develop multi-purpose service centers where clients can receive more than one type of service within the same building. The goal of such "one stop shopping" arrangements is to increase a homeless person's access to services. Homeless individuals may need, but not seek, more than one service, or be willing to go to more than one location. By offering multiple services at one site, agencies are better able to comprehensively meet the needs of clients.

VAGLAHS's Comprehensive Homeless Access Center

The VAGLAHS operates the Comprehensive Homeless Access Center for homeless veterans. VAGLAHS staff realized that homeless veterans had multiple needs and designed the Access Center to co-locate primary medical care, mental health, and homeless services. The structure of the access center dramatically changed "business as usual" for VA medical services. Now, a nurse conducts a complete bio-psycho-social assessment on clients including medical, treatment, and housing needs. The nurse will also review the person's history of using VA medical and homeless services within the LA system and the larger VA network. The veteran receives a comprehensive treatment plan addressing all bio-psycho-social issues including referrals to appropriate services. Referrals to services are then prioritized according to need.

Access Center clients receive same day appointments and immediate medications, which is very important to homeless individuals who may have difficulty keeping appointments. Homeless veterans can receive emergent, urgent, or routine medial care (such as physicals) the same day they access the center. Those needing emergent or urgent care are transferred to the VAGLAHS hospital on campus and those needing routine care are sent to the second floor of the building where the primary care facilities are based. The veterans shower and receive clean clothes before receiving medical care. Homeless veterans now have physicals the same day they come into the center as opposed to waiting six to eight weeks for a physical as they did before the center opened.

VAGLAHS staff members realize housing increases stability and stability increases the likelihood that veterans will follow up with additional medical services and appointments. Therefore, in addition to immediate medical care, homeless veterans accessing the center are directly linked to housing. Staff members find homeless veterans temporary housing in transitional programs that have openings in their collaborative network and are appropriate to the needs of the particular veteran.

Veterans experiencing severe psychiatric problems such as delusions or suicidal ideations are sent to the psychiatric emergency room. Otherwise, psychiatrists conduct same day assessments for those experiencing less emergent psychiatric problems. The clients are then referred to the mental health clinic's orientation program given provided weekly.

After the triage process described above, about 80 percent of the clients are referred to a social worker for more detailed assessments of complex issues. Together the veteran and social worker develop referral plans to address other needs, such as substance abuse treatment and social service needs. The social worker continues to provide case management and follow-up services with the Access Center clients as long as necessary. The Access Center also provides the first time user with a hot lunch from the campus cafeteria. There are plans to begin providing dental care to homeless veterans in summer 2003.

- **Seattle's Dutch Shisler Sobering Support Center.** The Sobering Support Center was built and is owned by Community Psychiatric Clinic and co-locates three connected programs collaborating to provide services for chronic public inebriates: the Sobering Support Center itself; the Emergency Service Patrol; and the REACH Project. The Sobering Support Center, funded by King County, cares for people as they sober up. Another county program, The Emergency Service Patrol, operates a van that picks up vulnerable homeless people from the streets and brings them into services. Sobering Support Center staff members refer clients to REACH, which provides case management services. REACH staff members target the most vulnerable and difficult to serve, who are likely to make heavy use of the Sobering Center. REACH workers assist clients to apply through the Department of Social and Health Services for state Alcohol Drug Abuse Treatment and Support Act funds, eligibility for which opens the door to all chemical dependency services in Seattle. This fund provides cash assistance to people who are disabled due to addiction as long as they are in treatment and have a payee. REACH also provides its clients direct links to housing, a good part of which grew out of CPC advocacy. A number of Seattle housing providers are more willing to take REACH clients because the project is well respected.
- For a person in King County to receive public mental health services, he or she must first be entered into the county's mental health database. The database, an outgrowth of ACCESS, tracks every client's mental health service use and also logs the agencies that provided the care. Several agencies dealing directly with street homeless people are part of this system. Because two agencies serving the same client cannot both receive reimbursement, the database is also used to prevent service duplication and encourages

some service coordination. Any agency interviewing a prospective new client will check with the database to see if the person is already in the system. If yes, staff will reconnect the person to the original agency or, if the person seems to prefer the new agency steps are taken to reassign the service responsibility. The database also provides opportunity for coordinating mental health services with local hospitals and jails, as these latter institutions can check the database and, if there is a provider of record, connect a person to that provider.

Processes to Alter Access to Mainstream Settings

Homeless individuals require many services and supports beyond what homeless service providers offer (Burt et al., 2002). Many of the services and supports are provided through mainstream agencies that do not specifically have a focus on homelessness, including mental health, substance abuse treatment, and social service agencies. HUD encourages communities to use mainstream agencies when serving homeless people. Mainstream agencies have increased involvement in serving the chronically street homeless population through new roles in old agencies and co-location of services.

Co-Location of Service Providers in Mainstream Agencies

One way that mainstream agencies have increased access to their own services and supports or access to other agencies' services for their own clientele is through co-location. Co-location is when staff members from one agency are located within the building of another agency to reduce barriers to services. For example, Seattle's Downtown Emergency Service Center has outreach staff located at the Department of Health and Social Services one day a week so eligibility workers can refer clients directly to the person for services if necessary. The Los Angeles County Sheriff's Department has created the Community Transitions Unit to empower jail inmates to be successful once they leave custody. Homeless veterans are one of the unit's target populations. The unit staff members contact VAGLAHS to verify veteran status of inmates prior to placement in the veteran portion of the facility. (Offenders can be in the veteran portion of the facility as long as they are not mentally ill or are not charged with murder or sex offenses. Mentally ill inmates are housed in a different portion of the facility). The VAGLAHS, US Vets, and the Salvation Army each have staff located in the facility to provide services and classes to veterans. Services include assessments for treatment, drug and rehabilitation classes, parenting classes, personal relationship classes, computer training, job skills, and resume building.

New Roles in Old Agencies

Some mainstream agencies in the communities we visited have altered their philosophy by accepting greater responsibility for serving chronic street homeless people. These agencies have reduced barriers and increased access to their services.

Philadelphia. The city Office of Emergency Shelter and Services (OESS) maintains two central intake systems, one for single men and one for women with or without accompanying children. Emergency shelter occupancy went from about 80 percent to 97 percent once the central intake system was fully operational. While it does not run any shelters or transitional programs itself, the city pays for shelter for all people that OESS places into emergency or transitional programs. The intake databases link to a management information system that can provide an unduplicated count and other information about people served, going back to 1989.

The Housing Support Center is a new program just getting under way within the city Office of Adult Services (AS). When fully operational, it will bring together resources from AS, Department of Human Services, Community Behavioral Health (CBH), the County Assistance Office (cash assistance), the Philadelphia Housing Authority (PHA), and other public agencies whose clients face challenges to housing stability. It will serve as the city's central referral point for all households needing help because they are experiencing homelessness or facing homelessness, including families whose involvement with child welfare arises chiefly from their lack of housing.

Agencies under Philadelphia's Behavioral Health System offer prevention, outreach, substance abuse, and mental health services through their own staff and by contracting with nonprofit homeless assistance programs. The Coordinating Office of Drug and Alcohol Abuse Programs and the Office of Mental Health are city offices whose staff provides care directly and who also pay for services and shelter/housing through contracts for people meeting their eligibility criteria. Both work closely with the outreach teams under the Outreach Coordination Center run by Project H.O.M.E., as well as supporting outreach teams of their own. Direct mental health and substance abuse treatment is also supplied through CBH, the city's nonprofit managed behavioral health care entity covering poor people with behavioral health disorders, whether Medicaid beneficiaries or not. All are components of Philadelphia's Behavioral Health System (BHS).

Los Angeles. The Department of Mental Health (DMH) Adult Systems of Care administers the AB 2034 program in Los Angeles County. AB 2034 is a state-funded program to address the mental health needs of persons whose illnesses have led them to homelessness and incarceration. In Los Angeles, these funds focus on providing appropriate supports to incarcerated people with serious mental illness, to prevent (return to) homelessness upon release. They thus link DMH and the County Sheriff's Department in a new and important partnership.

Several mainstream agencies cooperate in providing outreach for the program. Most AB 2034 clients enter the program from jail. When jail staff members identify a prospective AB 2034 client, they contact the Program Evaluator who begins the intake process into the AB 2034 program to determine program eligibility. At this point, the agency initiates the engagement process and remains connected with the client during incarceration. While in jail, the inmate is followed by one of two AB 2034 case managers who advocate for the client and work with the sheriff's department to produce an effective discharge plan. Referrals can also come from the courts, prosecutors, parole officers, county mental health programs, self-referrals and referrals from family members. The AB 2034 Program Evaluator works with police departments, prosecutors, and parole officers to negotiate alternative sentencing programs for inmates who qualify for the AB 2034 program.

The Adult Systems of Care's Housing Coordinator provides technical assistance to the agencies in leasing and purchasing housing and in completing applications for Section 8 housing vouchers. The Housing Coordinator also works with the Los Angeles City Housing Authority on a case-by-case basis to apply for exemptions for clients with criminal histories.

AB 2034 funds give Housing Specialists the flexibility to overcome property owner resistance by employing such innovative strategies as paying the rent until the client receives his/her housing voucher and placing an early deposit on a housing unit so the property owner will have funds available to make necessary repairs to bring the building up to Section 8 standards. The Housing Specialists can also intervene if an eviction is imminent or use AB 2034 funds to repair any damage done by the client. To recruit more landlords willing to rent to AB 2034 clients, the Department of Mental Health hosted a landowner/property owner breakfast for which they brought in speakers to speak on such topics as how to become Section 8 landlords and how to obtain low interest loans.

The Housing Specialists have made such an impact that some landlords have taken their names off the HUD Section 8 list and only rent to AB 2034 clients. Not only do the housing specialists provide technical assistance and temporary financial relief for Section 8 landlords serving their clients, but the AB 2034 clients come with case managers who resolve problems between tenants and landlords.

CONCLUSIONS

Housing First, safe haven, low demand, and harm reduction approaches, which usually occur in combination, appear to be very successful at attracting chronically street homeless people. Focus groups of street homeless people and outreach workers interviewed during site visits attest to their attractiveness, as do these communities' evidence of successful recruitment into permanent supportive housing and publicly available reports (Anderson et al., 2000; Rosenheck et al., n.d.; Shern et al., 1997; Tsemberis and Eisenberg, 2000). Chronically homeless disabled people *will* come in, they *do* use services even though not required to, they *do* reduce their substance use, and mostly they *do not* return to the streets.

In addition to the new approaches, making a commitment to ending chronic homelessness often means increasing the availability of existing programs and services that help people to leave homelessness. These might include increasing access to case managers, reducing case manager caseloads, expanding short- and medium-term addiction recovery programs (for those who will accept them) that fill gaps so people are not left without a program when they are not yet secure in their recovery, increasing availability of housing subsidies, and so on. It takes many components to create a successful system. Some will be new, others old. Birmingham, for instance, has some successful programs based entirely on sobriety and transitional rather than permanent supportive housing. But serious commitment to ending chronic street homelessness necessitates a paradigm shift, part of which involves the willingness of a community and its homeless assistance providers to consider approaches that have been proven to work even though they may, at least initially, represent a significant departure from traditional programs.

A number of agencies in the communities we visited have found innovative ways to address client needs. Some agencies do this within their own structure, such as through mini-continuums. Other agencies have accessed resources through other organizations in the community and developed structures where they interact to provide services to chronically street homeless clients. Many of the communities have collaborative relationships between agencies to serve this population such as those working in multi-agency teams, multi-agency special case teams, and multi-purpose service centers. Others have at least developed communication and coordination mechanisms to try to improve services for the chronically street homeless population. Many communities have also taken advantage of database technology to increase their interactions and knowledge flow perhaps thereby improving services for clients.

ASSEMBLING RESOURCES AND SUPPORTS

Once communities recognized that existing programs and services were not reducing or ending chronic homelessness, committed themselves to that goal, and identified potentially successful strategies, they still faced the task of assembling the resources and supports needed to implement their plan. In Chapter 2 we identified the sources of those supports—commitment and investment from mainstream agencies, the business community, local elected officials, and the general public. Each source may contribute interest, leadership, funding, staff, collaboration, and willingness to change.

Previous chapters have been organized by topic, illustrated by examples from several communities. In contrast, this chapter is organized by community to show how each community drew together the elements necessary to succeed. We first describe developments in two communities with long histories of cooperative investment in homeless programs and services—Philadelphia and Columbus. As will be seen, even these communities still had to make their case for new strategies and gather resources and supports. We then present two examples of developing new goals and strategies in the absence of any previous structure or commitment—San Diego and the Veterans Affairs Greater Los Angeles Healthcare System. Finally, we give an example of what has been accomplished in Seattle to assist chronically homeless people with mental illness and substance abuse problems, even without a change in the larger community toward a commitment to end chronic street homelessness.

Assembling Resources in Communities with Long Histories of Support

Philadelphia and Columbus are two communities with a very long track record of organized commitments to homeless assistance programs and services. Each already had an effective organizational structure, the commitments of local elected officials, extensive mainstream public agency involvement and investment, and general public support. Yet each still had to mobilize resources once it defined a new direction.

Philadelphia

Trigger Event. In 1998 a City Council member introduced a bill to criminalize many of the behaviors and actions of homeless street people. The proposed legislation galvanized the homeless advocacy community and brought a great deal of pressure to bear on the Council. The city ordinance eventually passed, but not before it had been changed in major ways and carried with it significant new funding to provide alternatives to street homelessness.

The response to the sidewalk behavior legislation was a remarkable example of what Philadelphia respondents mean when they say there is no progress without tension, "as long as we all still talk with each other." Downtown businesses wanted to do something to decrease the odds that people coming downtown to shop, do business, attend conventions, or visit tourist attractions would encounter panhandlers or people living on the streets. Advocates countered with two tacks—1) arresting people would just add a criminal record to their other difficulties in leaving homelessness, and 2) if you want to get people off the streets, you have to offer some alternatives that they are willing to take. The Open Door Coalition, a group formed in 1997 to develop viable plans for permanent long-term supportive housing for homeless individuals, solicited support from the media and community residents to protest the Sidewalk Behavior Ordinance in its original form.

After a good deal of controversy, and conversation, the results were:

- An ordinance passed, and is still city law.
- Proscribed sidewalk behavior is not criminalized, however. Instead, police may issue a ticket similar to a parking ticket, and then only after making several attempts to offer shelter or other assistance themselves, calling an outreach worker, and having the individual refuse any type of assistance from the outreach worker.

- New services were authorized to provide alternatives to living on the street, and about $5 million annually in new money was authorized to pay for them. The services include:

  ➤ The Outreach Coordinating Center (OCC), its management and oversight activities, and its outreach teams (see Chapter 3);
  ➤ Four new safe haven residences, comprising 85 new low demand beds for substance abusers, mentally ill individuals, and those with co-occurring disorders;
  ➤ New commitments to PSH.

- The police department established a special Homeless Outreach Team to work with OCC outreach and respond to street emergencies.

Mainstream Agency Involvement. As a conscious part of Philadelphia's approach to ending chronic street homelessness, many city agencies serve this population. Most use their resources to fund homeless assistance programs or supportive services and case management; many also offer some programs and services with their own staff. All participate in weekly and monthly meetings of city agency heads, and in one or more of Philadelphia's three citywide coordination mechanisms—the annual Strategic Planning Committee, the Blueprint to End Homelessness, and the Mayor's Task Force on Homelessness. Philadelphia's history in the homeless arena attests to its willingness and ability to entertain new ways of doing things when the situation warrants. The city began developing PSH in the early 1980s, long before McKinney funds became available for this purpose. In the early 1990s it served as a model and one of the sites for the Program on Chronic Mental Illness, a national demonstration of supported housing funded by HUD and the Robert Wood Johnson Foundation. Over the years the city has thoroughly changed its approach to outreach (from night to day, and much-increased coordination), and developed targeted responses to street homelessness in its no/low demand programs.

Private Sector Involvement. The Center City District, Philadelphia's downtown Business Improvement District, has been active since at least 1991 in addressing street homelessness, including providing jobs for homeless and formerly homeless people. Earmarking funding in response to the Sidewalk Behavior Ordinance to expand street outreach was in part a response to concerns of the business community. Street outreach has been crucial in helping homeless individuals move off the street; which met a business community objective to improve downtown visiting attractions. The Center City District's concern for street homelessness translated directly into funding and running an outreach team; its daytime outreach approach proved so useful that it became the model that Philadelphia outreach efforts now follow.

Committment from Local Elected Officials. The City Council supported and passed the revised Sidewalk Behavior Ordinance and approved additional funding for all of its provisions. The current mayor established the Mayor's Task Force on Homelessness even before he took office as another response to street homelessness. With almost 70 members representing every possible interested party, the Task Force addresses issues related to street homelessness, especially in the center city area. These issues include outreach, access to shelter resources, police/community/ homeless person relations, differentiating between panhandling and homelessness, running public education campaigns, services delivered "on the street," and similar issues. Members include representatives from the city council, businesses, faith communities, neighborhood and civic associations, homeless services providers, relevant government agencies, the Chamber of Commerce, legal and housing advocates, universities, the Convention Center and Visitors Bureau, the Center City District, and private foundations.

Role of Consumers in Advocacy and Shaping Policy. Homeless people themselves have been involved from the beginning in advocacy and actions to bring attention to the needs of people without shelter for the night. Homeless advocates have been very successful in rallying community support on the issues of homelessness in the political arena. For example, during the 1999 election of Philadelphia's mayor, homeless advocates formed a nonpartisan coalition called "Election '99: Leadership to End Homelessness," which educated the community through forums and workshops on the issues of homelessness, publishing and distributing more than 10,000 copies of the Voters' Guide on Homelessness and Housing, and registering over 2,000 homeless and low-income individuals to vote. Members of the coalition also organized a forum with the mayoral candidates, attended by more than 800 people, to examine the candidates' strategies for creating additional affordable housing units as well as obtaining their commitment to find solutions to end homelessness. The coalition has also been active in statewide senatorial and gubernatorial elections.

Columbus

Trigger Event. The Rebuilding Lives initiative grew out of a request by the City of Columbus in August 1997 for a plan to address the needs of people experiencing housing crises who were being affected by the development of the Scioto Peninsula, a riverfront corridor in downtown Columbus where many street homeless people congregated. In response to that request, the Community Shelter Board, with the support of the Franklin County Board of Commissioners, the City of Columbus, and United Way of Central Ohio, established the Scioto Peninsula Relocation Task Force, which issued the Rebuilding Lives plan in October 1998. The letter introducing the Task Force's report is addressed "To the Franklin County Community." Columbus views ending homelessness the responsibility of the entire community, not some smaller group such as the Community Shelter Board, homeless service providers, or elected officials. Launched in July 1999, the Rebuilding Lives initiative focuses on ending homelessness and 'rebuilding lives' by meeting the short-term needs of homeless individuals through an improved safety net of emergency shelters and by establishing 800 units of stable supportive housing programs for homeless individuals with long-term needs.

Mainstream Agency Involvement. A major focus of the original Rebuilding Lives plan was identifying and securing the resources needed for implementation. The plan outlines several options for new financial resources: establishing dedicated local revenue sources for broad-based affordable housing activities; encouraging innovative, entrepreneurial businesses tied to programs serving homeless individuals; and generating private, state and Federal funding for specific projects. Resources for Rebuilding Lives are managed through a specially created "Funder Collaborative" that allows individual funding agencies to pool their resources to achieve mutually agreed-upon goals, establish common expectations about what outcomes are to be achieved, and specify what reporting requirements are needed to document progress towards those goals. Funder Collaborative members include elected representatives of city and county government, all of the major public agencies, private agencies such as the Corporation for Supportive Housing, and philanthropic organizations such as the United Way and various local corporate donors. Key members are the Alcohol, Drug and Mental Health Board of Franklin County (ADAMH), which coordinates all community-based alcohol, drug addiction, and mental health services in Columbus; the Columbus Metropolitan Housing Authority; and the Departments of Job & Family Services and Health.

Mainstream agency commitment to the larger goals of Rebuilding Lives is clear from many actions, of which we describe only one here. Recognizing a gap in services for people with addictions who were not also mentally ill, the Maryhaven Engagement Center was designed and developed to improve on existing detoxification facilities and offer a more inviting entrée to services for male and female public inebriates. This is a population whose treatment is vital to the success of Rebuilding Lives. Funded by the Community Shelter Board, the ADAMH Board, and HUD support for safe havens, the Center has an overall capacity of 54 beds and provides overnight accommodations and services. Clients may remain in the Engagement Center for three days without receiving substance abuse treatment, or ten days if they participate in Maryhaven's outpatient detoxification program, which is right next door. Individual inebriates, however, can be admitted to the engagement center as often as needed. The usual stay is for one night. Once someone enters the Engagement Center, attempts are made to engage him or her in substance abuse treatment and other services working towards the goal of permanent housing.

Private Sector Involvement and Local Elected Officials Commitment. Rebuilding Lives has a great deal of community support and political backing, building upon the same elements in Columbus' long-standing commitment to addressing the issues of homelessness in a unified way through the Community Shelter Board. The executive director of the Community Shelter Board explained that both Columbus and Franklin County have high quality elected officials and the community has a long-standing tradition of caring about people, not just homeless people. The message is "bipartisan and very moderate— you don't have to support us because you like homeless people, you can just not like homeless people on the street in front of your business." Also, the business and political leadership mentors itself and ensures that this tradition of caring for and helping others continues over time.

Mobilizing Resources "From Scratch"

Two of the communities we visited provide examples of how resources and supports were mobilized when no prior structure of commitments or relationships existed that had a primary focus on homelessness. San Diego mobilized business community, mainstream agency, and ultimately political support for a commitment to end street homelessness in the downtown area, overcoming a long history of government disinterest and lack of cooperation between city and county government agencies and elected bodies. In Los Angeles, the history of the current collaborative network of public and private agencies serving homeless veterans reveals the roles of advocacy and political commitment in demanding a new goal and stimulating a public agency to devote the resources needed to reach it.

San Diego

The Role of Trigger Events. As downtown San Diego revitalized during the 1990s, the issue of street homelessness and what to do about it became a focus of discussion. In 1998, a camp-out by homeless advocates in front of the municipal building grew over the course of a few months from a few people to more than 300. Initially sent to remove the campers, the police department drew upon its problem-solving, community-oriented approach and sought a positive resolution. After interviewing campers, officers realized that the issues raised required responses beyond anything the police could muster, and began a process that ultimately produced San Diego's Homeless Outreach Team (see Chapter 3 and Appendix G).

Also in 1998, the decision was taken to build a new major league ballpark downtown, in an area that had become the most recent center of street homelessness. Anticipating displacement, residents in nearby areas began raising concerns about where homeless people would move next, while downtown businesses expressed concerns about "doing something serious" to reduce street homelessness. The impending ballpark development galvanized San Diego businesses and government agencies to get serious about reducing street homelessness in a responsible way.

Mainstream Agency Involvement. Interested parties from public agencies and the business community began meeting and soon constituted themselves the Ad Hoc Committee on Downtown Homelessness. The Committee serves as the major coordination mechanism for planning, assembling resources, and developing programs related to ending street homelessness. From the beginning of this response, the downtown redevelopment agency (Centre City Development Corporation—CCDC), businesses (the Downtown San Diego Partnership), the San Diego Police Department, and the courts were extensively involved, as were the city's housing authority (San Diego Housing Commission) and its Department of Community and Economic Development/Division of Homeless Services.

The Committee has no formal existence, which members say is its strength. Members described their initial process as "our approach was to sit around the table and ask ourselves what should our approach be." Committee members think their success is due to the many conversations they had, and their commitment to seeking information until they felt they knew what they wanted to do and something about how they wanted to do it. New agencies and stakeholders were invited to participate as it became clear to the first organizers that their roles were vital to success. The Committee's unbureaucratic and unofficial nature allows each participating agency and organization to be frank about its issues and tensions, as well as about its resources and abilities. Attendance by agency heads means that the power is present to make decisions, commit agency resources, and see that plans are carried to completion. Peer-to-peer accountability once commitments have been made keeps things moving forward, and peers can help troubleshoot bottlenecks and barriers and offer their own resources to help regain momentum if things do not work as expected.

A very significant addition to the San Diego effort was the opening of a regional office of the Corporation for Supportive Housing (CSH). It provides a team member that has full time staff focused on the issue of supportive housing. Courting the CSH to open an office in San Diego was an important achievement of the Ad Hoc Committee, and in turn the CSH presence adds strength and stability to the Committee's work.

Private Sector Involvement. CCDC works closely with the business community. The portfolio of one staffer includes responsibilities to "solve problems" in the downtown area, so homelessness fell into her bailiwick. In addition, the chair of the CCDC Board of Directors became very interested in the issue and provided essential leadership. The President of the Downtown San Diego Partnership, who was also an advocate for mentally ill homeless people and a political activist, played a key role in educating the business community and bringing it to the table. Guest speakers educated both Partnership and Ad Hoc Committee members about homelessness, the relation of mental illness and co-occurring disorders to homelessness, and best practices elsewhere in the state and country to address the needs of chronically homeless people.

Two people more than any others spearheaded San Diego City's activity on the Committee—one was a planner from the City Manager's office, and one was a private developer who was in charge of the ballpark development. The former, who estimates she spent about half her time for a year on the effort, is described as "the glue that kept it all together." They attribute their success in their roles to their neutrality—they started the process knowing nothing about homelessness or homeless programs, but being willing to learn and having no preconceived ideas. They went everywhere, asked endless questions, brought fresh perspectives to existing programs, and thought about "why couldn't we do X?" rather than "we've never done it that way."

The combination of their politics also helped—one was a liberal public servant, the other a conservative businessman. When both of them agreed on a course of action, they tended to carry the day with audiences across the political spectrum. By December 1999, the Committee's five-part program to assist the special needs homeless population had been presented to and approved by the San Diego City Council. Its parts included:

- Creating a centralized intake and referral system and locating a facility;
- Building transitional housing beds for special needs homeless people;
- Building permanent supportive housing units for special needs homeless people;
- Expanding residential alcohol and drug treatment programs for substance dependent and dually diagnosed homeless people; and
- Evaluating and expanding the Police Department's Serial Inebriate Program.

Commitment from Local Elected Officials. Part of the Ad Hoc Committee's success lies in drawing in players from both the city and county, in a spirit of cooperation that was unprecedented in San Diego up to that point. When the Committee was ready it asked for, and got, an historic, first-time joint meeting of the City Council and County Board of Supervisors. These two bodies committed themselves to the plans offered by the Committee and to working together to make them happen. This public commitment was an important policy progress. The City Council and Board of Supervisors created a Joint City-County Homeless Program Committee and appointed two members from each body to serve on it. These members in turn assigned staffers to work on the committee, which held regular meetings at which staff of city and county agencies reported progress toward various goals and discussed ways to reduce any barriers that arose. This Joint Committee became an important avenue through which city and county agencies could talk to each other and develop collaborative plans.

Los Angeles Veterans Affairs

The history of how the Veterans Affairs Greater Los Angeles Healthcare System (VAGLAHS) developed its current system is a dynamic example of how advocacy stimulated political commitment, which in turn changed public agency leadership and resource commitments. The result is a greatly changed and expanded system addressing the needs of many chronically homeless veterans who were not being served before. Developments began with increased communication—initially adversarial but changing to information gathering and open dialogue. The final system is fully collaborative, with each partner working together in newly developed ways to achieve the goal of ending homelessness for many disabled veterans.

Role of Advocacy in Developing Political Commitment. During the late 1980s and early 1990s, even the health services available to homeless veterans through VAGLAHS were limited, and only about six transitional housing beds were available. Homeless service providers and advocates appealed to the VAGLAHS administration and demonstrated on VAGLAHS' Los Angeles campus to obtain more services for homeless veterans. The group met resistance locally, which inspired them to go to Washington, DC to inform congressional leaders about the lack of services for homeless veterans. This movement resulted in a congressional hearing on the Los Angeles campus grounds, with representatives of VAGLAHS and community agencies giving testimony.

During the same time frame, staff from a community based organization, New Directions, wanted to begin providing services to veterans in one of the many empty buildings on the LA campus, but met great resistance to this idea. The organization worked to get an act of Congress to acquire a building on the campus, which occurred in 1989/1990.[17] The building is now the site of the New Directions South program.

Mainstream Agency Involvement. After the congressional hearing, VAGLAHS began to respond. The VA established a new administration at VAGLAHS in the early 1990s, and created a department focused on homeless services (McGuire, et al., 2001). VAGLAHS leadership began to communicate with agencies about what veterans needed and how to develop a collaborative to address those needs. To further complicate the VAGLAHS situation, the West LA Health Care Center was downsizing its inpatient health care services because of lowered resources at the same time that the VAGLAHS was trying to expand its homeless service approach.

Recruiting Partners. VAGLAHS leadership recognized that it needed community organizations to adequately serve chronically homeless veterans, who face many barriers to service. The VA proceeded to develop partnerships with community agencies from 1992 through 2000, creating a network that now includes 11 private and 7 public agencies in Los Angeles city and county. The network's goal is to assist veterans to leave the streets and lead productive lives by addressing four needs: (1) access to health care and treatment; (2) income from benefits and/or employment; (3) stable housing; and (4) support networks. The collaborative network approach is based on the premise that no single agency can provide comprehensive services to meet these four needs. The network includes programs that range from unstructured drop-in centers to treatment facilities. Private agencies have developed a total of 930 new transitional housing beds for veterans—up from the 6 beds that were available in 1992 and the largest number in the country connected to a VA facility.

Progress Without Community-Level Commitment to Ending Chronic Homelessness

We encountered some examples of important developments for the street homeless population even in communities without a central guiding vision at the community level of ending street homelessness. Some of these examples used Federal funding opportunities to promote significant service development and interagency cooperation. We give one example—Seattle's service structures that capitalized on participation in the Center for Mental Health Services' Access to Community Care and Effective Services and Support (ACCESS) demonstration program that began in 1993.

Seattle Program Structure Growing Out of ACCESS

A Federal funding opportunity had an important impact on Seattle's programs for the chronically street homeless population. Federal guidelines for the five-year ACCESS project, in which Seattle's Community Psychiatric Clinic and Downtown Emergency Services Center (DESC) participated, emphasized cross-agency systems and services integration. This gave strong impetus to Seattle providers and government agencies to develop outreach and engagement services for chronic street homeless individuals. Through its assertive outreach, ACCESS found new pockets of homelessness and helped chronic street homeless persons through the eligibility process for health and human services. It helped spark system innovations in Seattle and King County services, such as the merger of the mental health and chemical dependency divisions of county government and adding a housing specialist to this staff (now called the Mental Health, Chemical Abuse, and Dependency Services Division, King County Department of Community and Human Services). The demonstration findings persuaded county government that it should continue to fund programs such as those operated through ACCESS, which would avert public outlays for back-end services such as jail and hospital costs.

Service Development and Mainstream Agency Linkages. The Systems Design Workgroup formed within ACCESS to examine and recommend changes in system functions related to homeless mentally ill people. A Chronic Public Inebriates workgroup formed at the same time in response to a county executive request, and developed an action plan to create appropriate services and housing. When the mental health and chemical dependency divisions of county government merged in 1998, the two groups also merged, renaming the new entity the Chronic Populations Action Council (CPAC) in 2002. These groups pushed with ultimate success to develop a number of specialized services for the chronically street homeless population. These include the Harborview Medical Center Behavioral Health Crisis Triage Unit, the Mental Health Court, the Dutch Shisler Sobering Support Center, the REACH Project, the mental health detoxification enhancement project, the Emergency Service Patrol, and pre-recovery and recovery-oriented housing projects such as the Archdiocesan Housing Authority's Wintonia project and a new DESC housing project.

The Dutch Shisler Sobering Support Center operations and the mental health database, already described in Chapter 3, illustrate the complex inter-agency relationships that had to be developed to make these programs work, and that still continue to serve chronically homeless people today.

Private Sector Involvement. The Downtown Seattle Association, a local business association focused on downtown business community concerns including social service policy, provides leadership in the area of chronic street homelessness. This group helps garner support from neighbors and improve community relations for projects serving this population. Specifically, it supports DESC's work and has been instrumental in the development of the new pre-recovery housing project being designed by DESC.

CONCLUSIONS

The examples described in this chapter show how a central guiding commitment has helped the communities that have one to mobilize the resources and supports needed to fulfill their goal of ending street homelessness. They also show that mobilization is necessary whether or not a community habitually invests generously in homeless assistance programs and services. Changing one's paradigm means changing one's goals and adopting new strategies to achieve them. Either communities must find new resources to develop these new strategies, or they must redirect old resources. As no one likes to take money away from functioning programs, the price of political support from existing programs almost always means finding new resources. Communities with a history of strong support for homeless assistance may have a somewhat easier time convincing potential funders that the new direction is the right one, because their track record of responsible system management makes them a credible source of new information. But they still have to make the case, just as did people in San Diego and the Los Angeles VA once they had convinced themselves of the direction they wanted to follow. It is certainly possible to develop good programs, and even good cross-agency cooperation, without a central guiding vision, as some of the Seattle programs demonstrate. But it is not as easy, and the pieces may have a harder time retaining their "systemness" when the pressures that brought them together disappear.

DOCUMENTING PROGRESS

We sought out programs and communities that could document that their approaches were achieving progress in reducing chronic street homelessness. This evidence took several forms:

- Changes in the number of people found on the street from year to year;
- Increases in the number of chronically street homeless people who have moved into permanent housing;
- Reductions in costs of providing emergency health, mental health, and shelter services; and
- Reductions in days homeless, hospitalized, or incarcerated.

In presenting the evidence we gathered from the study, we do not want to create the impression that success was under community control if it only tried hard enough. Many factors may influence the level of homelessness in a community, no matter how organized or complete the efforts to end it. Interviewees in the communities we visited noted that factors tending to increase chronic homelessness included a poor economy and resulting unemployment, shutting down one or more large SRO hotels where poor single people had lived, closure of state mental hospitals, and persistently high housing costs. Furthermore, the study communities' were generally more successful than most at tapping into Federal and, to a lesser extent, state programs reducing chronic street homelessness. Non-local resources have played a significant role in supporting integrated, community-wide approaches involving mainstream agencies and permanent supportive housing. Spreading such approaches nationwide will entail Federal and state commitments.

Changes in the Number of People Found on the Street from Year to Year

Counts of street homeless persons are a basic method of determining changes in the number of people found on the street from year to year. A difficulty in such counts is ensuring that the numbers do not change because of variations in definitions and completeness of coverage. Street counts are much more valuable if they are done regularly using the same methods. If the territory covered changes from year to year, it is also most useful if analysts report a time series of data for the same area. For example, Seattle has extended the geographic coverage of its annual street count, but also reports changes over time within a fixed core area. Street counts are also more valuable to a community when they gather data that will help with service planning, such as individuals' characteristics and needs, and cover homeless individuals residing in shelters or other program housing.

Despite the difficulties in maintaining consistency of coverage, street counts are the most direct measure of reductions in chronic street homelessness. Philadelphia, Birmingham, Seattle, and Boston have all conducted a series of street counts that we judged to have sufficient coverage and consistency to allow comparisons over time. One of our standards was that persons in emergency shelters should be counted as homeless, but not persons in permanent supportive housing. These four communities collected and presented their data in a manner that met this standard, or from which equivalent statistics could be calculated. We also checked to see that there were consistent guidelines in place for dealing with situations such as people sleeping in cars and abandoned warehouses. Finally we were concerned that attention was paid to the issue of whether there were changes in the geographic area of coverage. While recognizing that these communities do not have perfect coverage or consistency in their street counts, we think they are useable, direct measures of street homelessness.

Philadelphia Counts of Street Homeless Persons

Street counts conducted by Philadelphia's Outreach Coordination Center between 1998 and 2003 indicate positive outcomes from developing alternatives to living on the streets, including safe havens and permanent supportive housing (see Chart 5.1). Since 1998, outreach workers coordinated through the OCC have conducted quarterly street counts over an area that includes all of downtown and west and southwest Philadelphia. Summer counts declined from 395 in 1998 to 228 in 2000. Since 2000 the count has increased, reaching 370 in 2003. Interviewees at the site attributed the increased street homelessness to a downturn in the city's economy. Also since 1998, however, over 300 PSH beds have been created which presumably kept the street count from going even higher as the economy worsened.

Chart 5.1
Counts of Street Homeless Individuals in Philadelphia, 1998-2003

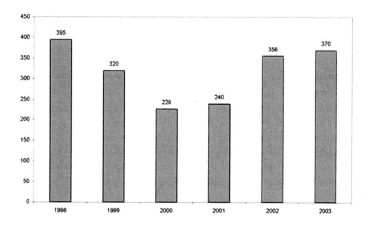

Birmingham Street Counts

Birmingham has done periodic counts of homeless persons complemented by a sample survey of the people counted. To provide a complete profile of the chronic homeless individuals in a community, a "street count" needs to go beyond the people on the street and include homeless individuals housed in emergency, transitional, treatment. Birmingham's counts provide a good example of the scope necessary. The number of homeless living on the street declined by one-third from 330 in 1995 to 220 in 2003, with most of the decline occurring between 1995 and 2001 (see Chart 5.2). This decline was achieved by "sheltering" and "housing" more people, because the sum of street homeless persons and homeless persons in programs providing shelter or housing increased from

1,404 in 1995 to 1,667 in 2001. By 2003 the sum of street homeless and persons in programs had declined slightly to 1,616.

Birmingham Street Counts

Birmingham has done periodic counts of homeless persons complemented by a sample survey of the people counted. To provide a complete profile of the chronic homeless individuals in a community, a "street count" needs to go beyond the people on the street and include homeless individuals housed in emergency, transitional, treatment. Birmingham's counts provide a good example of the scope necessary. The number of homeless living on the street declined by one-third from 330 in 1995 to 220 in 2003, with most of the decline occurring between 1995 and 2001 (see Chart 5.2). This decline was achieved by "sheltering" and "housing" more people, because the sum of street homeless persons and homeless persons in programs providing shelter or housing increased from 1,404 in 1995 to 1,667 in 2001. By 2003 the sum of street homeless and persons in programs had declined slightly to 1,616.

Chart 5.2
Counts of Street Homeless Individuals, Birmingham 1995-2003

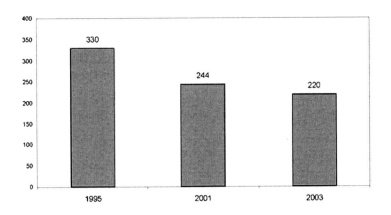

Street counts are a valuable tool for examining whether the total CoC system is succeeding in lowering homelessness, however, unless background history is collected one cannot determine what is behind the trends. A rising street count could be from many causes such as fewer individuals moving into housing, increasing migration of homeless individuals to the community, reduced state mental hospital beds forcing people with severe mental illness onto the streets, a new epidemic of substance abuse, declining housing for very low income individuals, increased job layoffs, or some combination of these and other factors. Birmingham's 2003 Homeless Survey included questions to shed light on the causes of homelessness. The survey also gathered information on age, sex, race, ethnicity, family status, education, income, veterans status, disabilities, health care, and homeless services being received. However, complete data on these other items are not yet available.

Seattle Street Counts

The Seattle/King County Coalition for the Homeless oversees an annual one night street count and survey of homeless shelters and transitional programs that have been conducted for 24 years (Seattle/King County Coalition for the Homeless, 2003). The survey of shelters and transitional programs is conducted the same night as the street count and produces unduplicated numbers of people using homeless services at the time of the count. The coalition returns annually to the same areas of the city and county to count street homeless individuals and also adds new neighborhoods to the count periodically. When comparing numbers of street homeless year after year, however, the coalition does some analyses that use a constant geographic area to avoid increases in numbers being attributable to the increase in area. From 1999 to 2002 the One Night Count of street homeless individuals went up 81 percent in "traditional count areas" from 983 to 1,779. From 2001 to 2002 the total count of street homeless individuals went up 40 percent from 1,454 to 2,040, but a substantial portion of that was from adding three new areas to the count. From 2001 to 2002, restricting the analysis to the 2001 geographic area, the number of street homeless individuals increased 23 percent in one year. From 1998 to 1999, during better economic times, a same geographic area count of street homeless individuals still went up 16 percent in one year.

During the 1999 to 2002 period, these increases in street homelessness occurred despite a 21 percent increase (from 4,917 to 5,940) in the survey count of the number of homeless individuals in shelter or transitional shelters. The community is losing ground while making improvements in resources for homeless individuals. One explanation is that homeless individuals are drawn to or sent to Seattle from surrounding communities. Our focus group of homeless individuals indicated that Seattle was known to be a relatively "good" place to be homeless. In the October 2002 One Night Count survey of shelters and transitional housing, 46 percent of the respondents indicated that their last permanent address was outside the City of Seattle. In the late 1990s there were skyrocketing housing prices in Seattle and some tearing down of single room occupancy buildings, and these economic pressures probably pushed more people on to the streets because they could not afford the available housing. More recently the job market has soured, and our interviewees reported that rising unemployment is also creating economic factors that result in more people being on the street. Even if people laid off do not become homeless, some may move to low rent quarters, making the affordable housing market tighter.

Of those using services in Seattle in 2002, 60 percent were single adults in shelter or transitional housing. Less than 1 percent used a safe haven. Forty-one percent of the homeless people using services were female and 38 percent were white (compared to 80 percent of the general population), 37 percent were African American (compared to 5 percent of the general population), 10 percent were Hispanic (compared to 3 percent of the general population), 5 percent were Native American (compared to 1 percent of the general population), and 4 percent were Asian/Pacific Islander (compared to 10 percent of the general population). The most frequently cited disabilities among homeless people using services were mental illness and chemical dependency.

The increase in Seattle's homeless population can be attributed to many challenges that overwhelmed the efforts of programs to tackle the issue of chronic street homelessness. Seattle has seen an economic downturn at the same time affordable housing has decreased. Indeed, individual program data from DESC, CPC, and AHA indicate these programs are successful in assisting chronically street homeless individuals into permanent supportive housing.

Boston Street Counts

Beginning in 1986 the ESC has conducted annual street counts in Boston with the assistance of over 250 volunteers who cover designated geographical areas in the city to enumerate homeless individuals sleeping on the streets and in the city's shelters and other homeless facilities. According to the December 2002 annual street count, the total number of homeless individuals residing on the streets of Boston and in adult emergency shelters has increased over the last decade:

The number of Boston's homeless increased by 41% in the past decade. There were 6,210 homeless people in the City of Boston in 2002 compared to 4,411 in 1992. There were 1,367 homeless children in Boston in 2002 compared to 800 in 1992, an increase of 71%. There were 1,572 homeless women in 2002 compared to 989 in 1992, an increase of 59%. There were

3,271 homeless men in 2002 compared to 2,622 in 1992, an increase of 25%. Although the number of homeless men rose at a slower rate than that of women and children, they remained the largest percentage of the population, 53%. The majority of these men have chronic disabilities such as mental illness and/or substance addiction (Menino, 2002, p.2). The increase in the number of homeless individuals can be traced directly to a number of conditions, including but not limited to:

- The dramatic rise in housing costs;
- The decrease of affordable housing for low-income persons;
- A reduction of substance abuse treatment beds; and
- A lack of commitment to aftercare planning and next step resources for individuals being released from jails and prisons, acute mental health facilities, hospitals, and social services.

In an effort to track the demographic information on homeless individuals, the city of Boston has contracted with the Center for Social Policy at the McCormack Institute, University of Massachusetts to implement Connection, Service and Partnership through Technology, which maintains the HMIS data system. Formerly known as the ANCHOR project, the HMIS data system is used by over 40 providers and enables Boston to collect and track unduplicated information on over 4,750 homeless individuals and 350 homeless families in Boston in order to provide unduplicated services and other resources needed to assist homeless individuals move towards self-sufficiency and permanent housing.

Last year, provider data revealed that at least 1,500 homeless people obtained permanent housing throughout the city of Boston, including 550 chronically homeless individuals. The Pine Street

Inn NBOR Project, which serves chronically street homeless people, reports that of 356 clients who exited the program in the past two years, 38 percent (134) obtained permanent housing and another 22 percent (77) were referred into a transitional housing program. The majority of clients in 2001-2002 were successfully placed into housing and more than 60 percent of them (103 of 171) entered housing after *more than four years of homelessness* (another 19 percent had been homeless between one and four years). The program achieved similar results more recently in 2002-03: 58 percent (108 of 185) of those housed had been homeless *from 4-6 years,* and 26 percent (48 of 185) had been homeless for 1-4 years. Most of the individuals successfully placed are repeat users of health care, mental health care, substance abuse, and shelter services and the locus of care and services simply shifted from the streets to fixed-site programs that served as a staging area for their successful placement into transitional and permanent housing.

Chronically Homeless Individuals Moved to Permanent Housing

Philadelphia Movement of Chronically Homeless Individuals into Permanent Housing

Permanent supportive housing is one avenue that may help chronically homeless people with disabilities move off the streets and into stable housing. We asked the major PSH providers if they had data that could document whether residents of their PSH units had been chronically homeless and whether they had achieved housing stability in PSH programs. Two providers, Project H.O.M.E. and Resources for Human Development (RHD), were able to provide relevant data.

Project H.O.M.E. provided data about residents in the four safe haven programs (with 80 beds) that are coordinated through OCC, and about residents in its five PSH projects (with 121 units) for single adults. Since inception, the safe havens have served 539 clients. All safe haven residents are either mentally ill, substance abusers, or both, as well as being likely to have other problems. Data on length of homelessness before entering a safe haven are available for 160 people, of whom 47 percent had been homeless for longer than 1 year, with 32 percent being homeless for 2 years or more. Among the 399 people for whom previous living situation is known, 30 percent came from the streets and other non-housing locations, 17 percent came directly from mental health or substance abuse treatment facilities, and 36 percent came from emergency shelters or a different safe haven. Among the 537 people whose length of stay at a safe haven is known, 52 percent stayed for 6 months or less, and 30 percent stayed for more than 1 year, with an average length of stay of 1.3 years. Information about current living situation is available for 516 people, of whom 23 percent still live at the safe haven, 36 percent moved to better housing situations (such as PSH, own housing, with family), 2.5 percent died; 22 percent left for situations that were similar or less desirable, and current whereabouts could not be ascertained for 18 percent.

Project H.O.M.E.'s PSH programs have served 187 people since July 1, 1999. Among the 122 people for whom length of previous homelessness is known, 67 percent had been homeless for one year or more, with 44 percent of these experiencing homeless spells of at least 2 years. Length of stay in PSH is available for all 187, among whom:

- 136 (73 percent) stayed for at least 2 years;
- 93 (50 percent) stayed for at least 1 year:
- 51 (27 percent) stayed less than 1 year; and
- The average length of stay was 3.2 years.

Of the 90 people who left Project H.O.M.E.'s PSH, current whereabouts are known for 86 percent. Of these, only 13 percent are living in situations that would be considered homeless, including on the streets, in emergency shelters, safe havens, or transitional housing programs. The rest are in a variety of stable housing situations.

RHD has served 121 consumers since 1995 in its Supported Adult Living Team (SALT) program and another 25 (since 1989) in its Boulevard Apartments. RHD provides supportive services to people with serious mental illness living in scattered-site residential units (SALT) or multi-unit building rent-subsidized apartments. Of these 146 consumers, 45 came directly from homelessness. Most of the remainder, all in the SALT program, had significant periods of homelessness although their immediately prior residence was various transitional housing situations. Of these 146 individuals, 72 percent stayed for one year or more, including:

- 61 (42 percent) who stayed for at least 2 years;
- 23 (16 percent) who stayed for at least 18 months but less than 2 years; and
- 21 (14 percent) who stayed for at least 12 but less than 18 months.

San Diego Movement of Chronically Homeless Individuals into Housing

San Diego's AB 2034 program for chronically homeless individuals with mental illness enrolled 404 persons between November 1, 1999 and January 31, 2003 in permanent supportive housing. It offered people immediate housing in a variety of settings, using hotels in the early period before safe haven and PSH slots became available. At the end of this period, 253 were still enrolled and 154 had been disenrolled for various reasons (59 percent of the 154 "disenrollees" dropped out of the program and another 17 percent moved out of the REACH program area).

Presumably most clients should be staying in permanent housing for a long period. If too large a percentage disenrolls, the program is having problems. Agencies can use simple length of stay in permanent housing to make some assessment of how a system is working. If the typical length of stay is six to eight months in a program designed to provide years of residence, the support services may be insufficient or the program may be taking in clients who do not need that high a level of care and are moving on to independent living. However, this does not appear to be a problem for the PSH programs we visited. Far more often providers noted that turnover among clients was much lower than expected, even after years of residence. Some communities are now beginning to think about lower-intensity options for tenants who have been stabilized for several years.

Birmingham Movement of Chronically Homeless Individuals into Permanent Housing

The Cooperative Downtown Ministries (CDM) has placed 189 persons into its transitional housing program since 2000. When placed about 80 percent were chronic street homeless individuals, 85 percent were substance abusers, 33 percent had a serious mental illness, and about 23 percent were dual diagnoses. The transitional housing program's capacity was 30 individuals, but has recently been expanded to 87. Of the 189 persons who have been in the program, 17 percent are still there, 49 percent left for permanent housing, 19 percent have unknown whereabouts (most are thought to be in housing with family or friends), 10 percent went to another program or jail and 5 percent left the program for other reasons.

The CDM opened its own PSH program only a few months ago, but has been placing people from its transitional housing program into other PSH programs. Many others have been connected directly to other permanent housing programs by CDM shelter's case manager without going through CDM's transitional housing program. Of the 75 who went from its transitional housing program to a permanent supportive housing program, 47 percent have remained at least 24 months, 21 percent at least 18 months, 13 percent at least 12 months and 19 percent less than 12 months.

Reductions in Costs of Providing Emergency Health, Mental Health, and Shelter Services

In Columbus existing shelter data indicate a 7 percent decrease in the total number of clients sheltered in 2001 as compared to 1998 (note these are all homeless clients, not just those who are chronically homeless). Of the 2,959 clients sheltered in 2001, 298 had successful outcomes, meaning they exited the shelter system to either permanent or transitional housing. The average length of stay during this period of time remained relatively stable for men, while it increased by over 20 percent for women, increasing from 37 days in 1998 to 47 days in 2001. During this period of time the recidivism rate increased by 14 percentage points for men and 3 percentage points for women.

Despite the limitations of the HMIS, the Community Shelter Board has been collecting extensive data on its homeless service system for many years, data that have guided both program and policy development in Columbus. These data have been used to evaluate the costs of running various Rebuilding Lives programs The two-pronged strategy at the heart of the plan (emergency housing for those in crisis and supportive housing for those with long-term needs) was largely a response to the fact that chronically homeless people (a group that accounts for only 15 percent of all those in need of homeless assistance) were absorbing the bulk of the community's homeless assistance resources. The Task Force recognized that the needs of this high-cost group could be met much more effectively, and at a lower cost, by providing them with permanent housing with supportive services. Table 5.1 is drawn from the Task Force's initial report:

Table 5.1 Per-Bed Costs for Operations and Services of Franklin County Service Systems Used by Homeless Men with Long-Term Needs

Service System	Annual Cost per Bed	Daily Cost per Bed
Service-Enriched Housing	$13,000-14,000	$36-38
Minimum Security Misdemeanor Jail	$ 21,188	$58
Sub-acute Medical Detox	$ 69,800	$191
State Psychiatric Hospital	$172,900	$482
Hospital Inpatient	$396,025	$1,085

With these figures in mind, the Community Shelter Board, service providers and funders, launched the initiative in July 1999.

In Philadelphia as elsewhere, 10 to15 percent of shelter users are absorbing half or more of shelter resources, at significant public expense. The idea that these people could be moved to housing and helped to maintain it through supportive services is appealing, in that it would help people leave the streets and save emergency shelter resources for true emergencies. In

Philadelphia at present the city pays for about 2,100 shelter beds a night, comprising about 80 percent of the city's emergency shelter capacity. This number is down about 10 percent from 2001, reflecting the deliberate effort to switch occupancy from emergency to permanent supportive housing for chronic shelter users. Philadelphia is just starting its first program based on a pure "Housing First" approach, bypassing even the safe haven stage of moving from street to housing. Research evidence on housing first models has convinced officials that this is an important model to try.

In San Diego the Serial Inebriate Program (SIP) did a cost analysis showing the very high levels of public resources being absorbed by serial inebriates, compared to the costs of treatment. They calculated a cost of $977 for maintaining one serial inebriate in housing plus outpatient substance abuse treatment for one month, compared to $1,470 for the cost of one police contact with an ambulance visit to the emergency room followed by a day in jail. The SIP participants were all people with very long histories of addiction and street homelessness, and all were treatment resisters. Nevertheless, over 3 years the program has an average annual completion rate of over 40 percent compared to average completion rates for voluntary substance abuse treatment programs for homeless people of between 20 and 33 percent, with most falling at the lower end (Orwin et al., 1994).

Also in San Diego the Homeless Outreach Team (HOT) Program asked the UCSD Medical Center to track care received by 15 mentally ill chronically homeless individuals well-known to the HOT workers at Scripps Mercy Hospital, UCSD Medical Center, and the San Diego emergency medical services system during an 18 month period from July 1, 1997 through December 31, 1998. The 18-month cost just for these 15 individuals was just under $1.5 million, which did not include physician fees or care that might have been incurred at other regional hospitals. UCSD physician charges totaled $87,017 for both in- and outpatient care for these same individuals during the study time period. HOT's expenditures of $69,820 a person a year to get chronic street homeless people with multiple disabilities into stable housing situations are close to the medical expenditures noted above, which would be $67,000 a person a year. If the costs of other public services such as law enforcement were added to the equation, HOT expenditures might be substantially offset by savings to other agencies, at least for the HOT participants who were high consumers of these services.

Among the communities we visited for this study, few had conducted cost avoidance studies of any complexity. Those we just documented form San Diego are fairly simple, yet have been effective in raising public consciousness that "doing nothing" is not free and that there may be better ways to invest public money, with more humane consequences as well as more livable downtowns. In recent years, several studies examining public crisis costs avoided as a result of offering permanent supportive housing or other service alternatives have been published and have excited national attention. The most prominent of these, by Culhane, Metraux, and Hadley (2002), was a key stimulant to development of national policy urging an end to chronic homelessness. Other similar analyses have been conducted for PSH programs in Connecticut (Anderson et al., 2000) and San Francisco (Martinez and Burt, 2003; Proscio, 2000). The most recent entry in the field is a three-year follow-up study of homeless veterans in a joint program of HUD and the VA that randomized assignment to housing plus case management versus just case management versus "usual services" (Rosenheck et al., 2003). The results of most of these studies show that a considerable proportion of the costs of PSH and supportive services may be compensated for by savings stemming from reduced use of public crisis services such as emergency rooms and public hospitals.

Reductions in Days Homeless, Hospitalized, or Incarcerated

In San Diego among the 253 formerly homeless clients currently enrolled, REACH had the following impacts, annualized to represent the 12 months before compared to the 12 months after enrollment, current enrollees have:

- 73 percent fewer homeless days;
- 55 percent decrease in incarceration days, and 71 percent decrease in incarceration episodes;
- 35 percent decrease in hospital days, and 62 percent decrease in hospitalization episodes; and
- 506 days of enrollment, on average, or about 1.4 years, in a program that in January 2003 had only been at full enrollment for about 2 years; 55 percent had been enrolled at least one year.

The Los Angeles AB 2034 program can show statistics with similar impacts, as can the program statewide. In Fiscal Year 2002-2003 the state expenditures for the program were $55 million, but the state estimates that at least $27 million was saved by the reductions in utilization of other services (Davis, Johnson and Mayberg, 2003). Programs providing these statistics are one of the reasons the program has been funded for the current fiscal year at the same level, despite the extreme state budgetary pressures (Davis, Johnson and Mayberg, 2003). In the Veterans Affairs Greater Los Angeles Health System (VAGLAHS), increasing housing options for homeless veterans, along with other changes in the system, helped to reduce the length of stay in medical, surgical, and psychiatric beds between 1994 and 1998 (McGuire, et al., 2001). The length of stay was reduced in medical beds by 28 percent, in surgery beds by 7 percent, and in psychiatric beds by 35 percent. Not only are programs assisting the VAGLAHS in decreasing the length of stay in their treatment and medical facilities, but the programs have also assisted the facility so they are not discharging patients to the streets, from which they will quickly cycle back. Both community program and VAGLAHS representatives report that the collaborative allows them to serve veterans better, and in a more cost-effective manner.

CONCLUSIONS

The primary ways that our study communities documented the progress of their approaches were through counts that showed reductions in the number of street homeless individuals, increases in the numbers of chronic homeless individuals being moved into permanent supportive housing, reductions in the costs of providing emergency services to homeless individuals, and decreases in the number of days that clients spent homeless, hospitalized or incarcerated. However, documenting progress is not an easy or straightforward process. None of the data described above is readily available in most communities. Furthermore, a community may have programs that are functioning well, but still have outcome measures, such as street counts, that are showing undesirable trends because of increases in the homeless population being driven by external events like slumps in the economy and/or reduction in state facilities for the mentally ill.

HOW COMMUNITIES PAY FOR THEIR NEW APPROACHES

Introduction

Funding is, of course, the fuel that propels programs and services for ending chronic street homelessness. Housing is the single resource that does the most to end homelessness for chronically homeless and other homeless people alike. Housing is generally expensive to create and, because rent subsidies are likely to be a long-term need, expensive to help people occupy. Add to the costs of the housing itself the costs of the supportive services that help chronically disabled people maintain housing, and it is evident that most commonly used approaches to ending chronic street homelessness require a good bit of funding. The cost of permanent supportive housing has prompted researchers and advocates to show that leaving chronically disabled people homeless is far from free, by identifying the costs of public crisis services used by chronically homeless people who do *not* have permanent supportive housing (Andersen et al., 2000; Culhane, Metraux, and Hadley, 2002; Martinez and Burt, 2003). As these costs have proven to be virtually as high as the costs of the programs themselves for severely disabled former street people, more communities are recognizing the value to public health and wellbeing of reducing street homelessness through providing housing and supportive services.

This chapter describes funding streams that communities use to support services and housing to end chronic street homelessness. The communities we visited have different resources available and therefore take different approaches to funding for this population. Some communities such as Philadelphia, San Diego, and Boston have access to a great deal of local and state funding, compared to what is typically found nationwide, which makes a difference in how they can tackle street homelessness. Communities such as Birmingham, however, have to be more creative in finding resources because they have far fewer state or local supports.

We first explore local, state, and Federal sources of funding that at least some of our seven communities have called into use to serve the chronically street homeless population. Additionally, we describe the ways in which communities use and blend resources to help both providers and clients. Provider overload is eased by "funnel agencies" that assemble monies from various sources and allow providers to write one application to access different funding streams. Client access to services is enhanced by providers with multiple funding sources that allow them to serve clients regardless of insurance status, and bill the care to the appropriate payors.

Local Funding

The communities in this study used local funding such as general revenue, special taxing mechanisms and private sector resources to help finance the cost of programs to reduce chronic homelessness.

General Revenue Resources

All the communities we visited invest some local general revenues in homeless assistance. Most target some of these resources specifically to efforts directed at reducing chronic homelessness. We highlight two communities here—Boston and San Diego.

Boston has substantial local public resources committed to serving the homeless population. It focuses on solving its affordable housing crisis and expanding affordable housing for low-income and homeless individuals and families. The mayor and the Strategic Homeless Planning Group (SHPG) have developed a three-year strategic plan, Leading the Way, to build 7,500 new affordable housing units (3,200 of these will be in new affordable developments or in reclaimed public housing now vacant) and to preserve 10,000 units of existing affordable housing. The city is contributing over $30 million plus city-owned land to achieve the plan's goals. To date, 34 percent of the city's affordable housing units are targeted to low-income households (those earning less than 50 percent of Area Median Income). While this income level is far higher than formerly street homeless individuals are likely to attain, easing the affordable housing crunch on all low-income households reduces the odds that these households will ultimately contribute to the homeless population through housing crises.

The City of **San Diego** funds outreach services—the Homeless Outreach Team (HOT) and the Serial Inebriate Program (SIP)—through its police department, as described in Chapter 3. These programs have a high success rate and recover their costs by reducing expenditures on arrests, transportation, bookings, detox, and emergency services.

City, county, and state money support San Diego's REACH program, which we describe in Chapter 3. The San Diego Housing Commission helps fund most of the housing portion of the program while the state-funded AB 2034 program supports mental health and other services through a flexible funding pool that will cover "whatever it takes." The county and city contract with non-governmental agencies to provide case management and supportive services.

Special Taxing Mechanisms

Several of our communities had the advantage of funding for housing development and operations through special taxing mechanisms created by state or local law. In addition to housing trust funds that are becoming more common throughout the country, we found some interesting mechanisms whose proceeds were being used to create permanent affordable housing for formerly street homeless people—tax increment financing in San Diego, a housing tax levy in Seattle, redevelopment bonds in Philadelphia, and general revenue bonds for mental health and substance abuse services in Columbus.

Tax increment financing. San Diego's downtown redevelopment agency, Centre City Development Corporation (CCDC), helps to create new developments and economic activity, generating new tax revenues for the jurisdiction. California law stipulates that the redevelopment authority receive back a share of these additional taxes (called tax increments), and says that the authorities must invest at least 20 percent of the money they get back to increase affordable housing (tax increment financing, or TIF). CCDC invests these funds in affordable housing projects, and has chosen to require some of them to set aside about one-fourth of their units for permanent supportive housing for the special needs street homeless population.

Property tax levies. Two of our communities, Seattle and Columbus, make significant use of voter-approved property tax levies to support housing and services, some of which benefit people who are or have been chronically homeless.

Seattle has a long history of voter-approved tax measures to finance low-income housing and housing for homeless people. Voters approved housing levies in 1981, 1986, 1995, and 2002. The 2002 housing levy totals $86 million over seven years with the cost to the average homeowner of $49 per year.[18] The program includes five major initiatives plus administrative costs: rental preservation and production (provides housing to people with disabilities, elderly, homeless, and working families and resources for rehabilitation, new construction, or redevelopment of units); home ownership for low-income working families; neighborhood housing opportunity program with a mixed income, mixed use emphasis; rental assistance to prevent homelessness; and operating and maintenance (for rental units for extremely low-income individuals and people with disabilities).

In Columbus, the Alcohol, Drug and Mental Health Board of Franklin County (ADAMH) coordinates all community-based alcohol, drug addiction, and mental health services for the city and county, including those addressing the needs of street homeless people and formerly homeless people now in permanent supportive housing. Almost half of the ADAMH system's resources are drawn from a single property tax levy (approved by voters); the remainder comes from state, Federal, and private sources. ADAMH does not provide any direct services, but contracts with a network of 45 public and private health care agencies to treat people in need.

Redevelopment bonds. Philadelphia's Redevelopment Authority recently obtained City Council approval for about $300 million in redevelopment bonds. Proceeds are being used to fund property acquisition and demolition as part of the mayor's Neighborhood Transformation Initiative. Some part of the housing being developed will be used for permanent supportive housing for formerly homeless disabled people. A much larger proportion will be used to preserve existing affordable housing and create more.

Use of Private Sector Resources

Given the paucity of public funding for homeless programs and services in Birmingham, providers have developed a number of approaches that build on the resources and interests of the private sector. Two nonprofit agencies that develop transitional and permanent housing (with and without supports) have had success approaching owners of dilapidated and wholly or partially vacant properties to see if they will donate the property. If they will, the agencies use capital financing from the Federal Home Loan Bank and private lenders, plus Low Income Housing Tax Credits, HOME funds, and donations from religious congregations and private individuals to renovate and make repairs. Property owners get tax write-offs on properties that were losing money and causing problems, the agencies get free buildings they fix up and use, neighborhoods get renovated and supervised buildings in place of eyesores and problem spots (not only not a NIMBY response, but a warm welcome), and participants in homeless job training programs gain construction skills as well as a sense of ownership as they prepare the housing for occupancy—perhaps by themselves.

State Funding

California and Massachusetts have extensive state funding programs for homeless-related programs and services and affordable housing. Ohio, Pennsylvania, and Washington have less extensive state funding but still have some state-level resources used by providers in the communities we visited.

California

AB 2034. California has a unique source of funding for homeless people, probationers, and parolees experiencing serious mental illness (Mayberg, 2002). Funding is authorized through Assembly Bills (AB) 34 (for the pilot year) and 2034 (for the first year of full funding) and is referred to as the AB 2034 program. The Department of Mental Health (DMH), Adult Systems of Care administers this program to provide community mental health services and outreach to mentally ill adults and transition-age adults who are homeless or at risk of homelessness, with the intention of preventing or ending their homelessness. In addition to homelessness, this population often experiences costly incarcerations and hospitalizations because their needs are not addressed until they are in crisis.

AB 2034 programs participate in a mandatory statewide evaluation that documents their impact. Statewide, the program has reduced hospitalization experiences; client data show a 66 percent decrease in hospitalization days statewide from the 12 months before to the 12 months after AB 2034 enrollment. Findings also show that about 60 percent of the clients are dealing with substance abuse issues in addition to mental illness and that once enrolled about 84 percent of clients continue in the program. Participation in AB 2034 services has reduced incarceration experiences, including the number of unduplicated clients who become incarcerated, the number of incarcerations overall, and the number of days incarcerated (82 percent fewer incarceration days statewide in the 12 months following enrollment compared to the preceding 12 months).

As of the 2002 report, California has spent $55 million overall on the AB 2034 program, or $13,000 annually per client statewide, meeting about 10 percent of the need according to county informants. This expenditure has been offset by $23 million in cost savings as a result of reduced inpatient hospital stays and reduced incarcerations. Two cities we visited have AB 2034 programs—Los Angeles and San Diego.

Other California funding streams. California has several other important state programs that communities use to fund programs to end chronic street homelessness and to create affordable housing. These include (Corporation for Supportive Housing, 2001):

- Supportive Housing Initiative Act (SHIA). SHIA, a program of the Department of Mental Health, encourages development of permanent, affordable housing with supportive services that enables low-income Californians with disabilities to stabilize their lives. It covers services and operating costs (through rent subsidies) in supportive housing. Funding was about $20 million a year, but renewal funds have not been available the past two years and many grants have expired.. It may become an important source of funding again when the state budget is not facing crisis deficits.

- Multifamily Housing Program (MHP). MHP, a program of the Department of Housing and Community Development, provided streamlined, omnibus permanent financing program for affordable multifamily housing development for special needs and disabled households, including homeless persons or persons at risk of becoming homeless. It provides low-interest loans to developers of affordable housing for new construction, rehabilitation, acquisition and rehabilitation, or conversion of nonresidential structures. Rent write-downs may be added in future years. Passage of Proposition 46 in California in November 2002 created a special Supportive Housing Program under MHP, which is for homeless or at-risk households with a disabled adult member. The funds total $190 million available over 3 years. Proposition 46 also expanded the amount of funding for the General Program to $770 million over 4 years.

- Special Needs Affordable Housing Lending Program. This program, under the California Housing Finance Agency, Multifamily Programs section, is designed to serve special needs populations by reducing interest rates (to 3 or 1 percent, depending on tenant targeting) on multifamily loan products to develop projects that serve low-income disabled tenants in need of special services to create stable, long-term supportive housing environments.

- Emergency Housing Assistance Program (EHAP). A program of the Department of Housing and Community Development since 1993, EHAP funds emergency shelter, transitional housing, and services for homeless individuals and families, including safe haven/low demand programs. Funds are distributed to all counties based on a formula that combines poverty and unemployment statistics. Funding fluctuates, usually between $10 and $20 million a year.

- Low-Income Housing Tax Credits (LIHTC). California augments Federal LIHTC with its own program to encourage private investment in affordable rental housing. The state program supplements Federal tax credits in projects that are eligible for them. In 2002 state funds were actually greater than Federal funds-- about $70 million added to the Federal $59 million.

Other State Funding Streams

Other sites we visited also have significant sources of state support. Boston has substantial state funding for homeless services. Massachusetts'

Departments of Public Health and Mental Health combined invested about
$31 million of mainstream funding to services for the chronically street
homeless population. Philadelphia receives support from Pennsylvania's
Homeless Assistance Program, mostly for families and thus not particularly
useful for the street homeless population that is the focus of this report. The
Washington State Housing Trust Fund and the Washington State Housing
Finance Commission (tax credits for constructing transitional housing),
provide funding support for emergency shelter and transitional housing
acquisition, rehabilitation, and construction in Seattle.

Federal Funding Other Than McKinney

Programs funded through the McKinney-Vento Act are the most
common Federal funding sources for the agencies serving the chronic street
homeless population. McKinney programs administered by HUD support
emergency services and transitional and permanent supportive housing.
Programs funding emergency services include the Emergency Shelter Grants
program (which HUD distributes by formula to eligible jurisdictions) and the
Emergency Food and Shelter Program (which a special board of the Federal
Emergency Management Agency distributes by formula to eligible
jurisdictions). Several funding streams support transitional and permanent
supportive housing, including the Supportive Housing Program (transitional
and permanent), Shelter Plus Care (permanent), and Section 8 Moderate
Rehabilitation SRO. Other large McKinney programs include Health Care
for the Homeless (administered by the Health Services Research
Administration within DHHS), Projects for Assistance in Transition from
Homelessness (administered by the Center for Mental Health Services within
DHHS), education for homeless children (administered by the Department of
Education), and several programs for homeless veterans (administered by the
Department of Veterans Affairs. From time to time, McKinney has also
included other programs and special research and demonstration projects.

While most homeless assistance providers and planners are aware of the
homeless-specific funding streams included in McKinney, the communities
we visited also used many other Federal sources of funding that might not be
so obvious to other communities. Table 6.1 shows all the Federal funding
streams appropriate to the task of reducing or ending chronic street
homelessness that are used for that purpose by the communities we visited.
A number of communities use various block grants—including Community
Development, Mental Health, Substance Abuse, and Preventive Health—to

support housing and services for chronically street homeless individuals. Using Seattle as an example, King County uses CDBG funding to acquire and rehabilitate rental units for homeless persons. Seattle uses CDBG funding to operate emergency shelter, transitional housings, and day/hygiene centers. The city also uses MHBG funds to administer involuntary treatment to clients who have included an unknown number of homeless individuals. In 2003 MHBG funds will also be used to fund HOST (an outreach program for street homeless individuals) and the Crisis Triage Unit in Harborview Medical Center Emergency Room. King County uses SABG funds to support county services to homeless individuals, including the Emergency Services Patrol that provides chronic public inebriates with transportation to the Sobering Center or the Crisis Triage Unit. Also, both Seattle and Philadelphia were part of the ACCESS demonstration program for homeless services through the Substance Abuse and Mental Health Services Administration, Center for Mental Health Services (DHHS).

The Veterans Affairs Greater Los Angeles Healthcare System's collaborative network of services uses a number of Federal funding streams to finance its work. Many of the community- based organizations that are part of the network receive funding through the VA's Grant & Per Diem program. Each partner agency applies directly to the VA for the grant.

The network also takes advantage of funding from the HUD-VA partnership known has HUD-VASH (VA Supported Housing). These funding sources do not appear in Table 6.1 because we did not do a funding table for Los Angeles as a whole. However, other communities should know about funding opportunities for homeless veterans available through the Department of Veterans Affairs.

One Birmingham provider gets loans through the Federal Home Loan Bank to renovate structures to create transitional and permanent supportive housing, and affordable housing without supportive services. Boston providers have also used this source of capital funds.

Five rows in the table have no entries: HOPE VI, Section 202, Section 811, Preventive Health BG, and Medicare. Although none of the communities reported using them, these are programs that can be used, and we are leaving them in to draw attention to their potential contributions.

Table 6.1: Federal Sources Invested in Ending Street Homelessness

Type of Investment	Site Visit Cities					
	Birmingham	Boston	Columbus	Philadelphia	San Diego	Seattle
McKinney-FEMA		X	X	X		X
McKinney-ESG	X	X	X	X	X	X
McKinney-SHP	X	X	X	X	X	X
McKinney-S+C	X	X	X	X	X	X
McKinney-SRO Mod Rehab		X	X	X		
HOPWA	X	X	X	X	X	X
HOPE VI-relocation and supportive services						
HOME	X	X	X	X	X	X
Section 811						
Section 202						.
Public housing units			X	X	X	
Section 8 (other than S+C)	X	X	X	X	X	X
Moving-to-Work (PHAs)				X		
CDBG	X	X	X	X	X	X
LIHTC	X	X	X	X	X	
Federal Home Loan Bank	X	X		X		
TANF-Services or MOE			X	X		X
SSBG				X		
MHBG		X	X	X		X
PATH		X	X	X		X
SABG		X	X	X		X
Preventive Health BG						
Health Care/Homeless	X	X	X	X	X	X
Medicaid		X	X	X	X	X
Medicare						
Workforce Investment Act (WIA-DOL)						
Homeless Veterans Reintegration Project (DOL)		X		X		
Department of Veterans Affairs	X	X	X	X	X	

Notes: Funding information is not included for Los Angeles because no central system was studied.

Self Support

Some programs use client contributions to fund aspects of their services or housing. Programs with particular focuses on job readiness, training, and employment, usually for recovering substance abusers, require client contributions of some sort once the person is employed. For example, all of the agencies in Birmingham offering shelter and housing use client wages for rent once the client has a job, and the programs work very hard to get people ready for work and help them find jobs. Providers say they have little trouble placing people in employment, and have a large network of job opportunities because they cultivate employers. Rents for emergency shelter are relatively low, but for transitional housing they come close to market rate, in part because there are few alternative sources of housing support, and in part because tenants are ultimately expected to become independent and conditions in transitional programs are set to create incentives for them to do so. In Los Angeles, tenants in the Westside Residence Hall (a partner in the Veterans Affairs Greater Los Angeles Healthcare System collaborative network) also pay rent if employed.

Funds Blending and Access

One of the biggest problems for homeless assistance providers is assembling the funds to be able to offer all the various services that chronically street homeless people with disabilities are likely to need. Few funders cover them all, so the challenge for providers is to keep track of which sources will fund what, when one needs to apply for them, who is eligible for services from particular funding streams, and who has time to do the applications. People at every level of government and service provider talk about "funding silos" and "categorical funding" that inhibits getting clients what they need. It is no wonder that providers value funding programs such as California's AB 2034, which can fund "whatever it takes" to end homelessness and prevent its recurrence. For homeless consumers, blended funding is also a boon. We highlight several approaches to providing wrap-around services through creative funding "funnels" at the consumer level.

Blending Funding from the Provider Perspective

In the absence of universal programs such as AB 2034, some communities have developed mechanisms that reduce the burden on providers by streamlining the funding acquisition process. We call these "funnel mechanisms" because, in theory at least, all the funding sources go in at the top, get blended, and come out at the bottom in single grants to providers to cover their program requirements. We found several examples of funnel mechanisms in the communities we visited, ranging from single requests for proposals (RFPs that offer blended funding from several agencies, arranged through memoranda of understanding among the funders) to routine funneling activity.

One-Time RFP. Agencies in San Diego are working to increase access to funding resources for homeless service providers by blending different funding sources. In 2002, the Centre City Development Corporation, the City of San Diego, Corporation for Supportive Housing, County of San Diego, and the San Diego Housing Commission (the city's public housing authority) developed a memorandum of understanding among themselves outlining resource and other commitments, and issued a first-ever joint request for proposals. This RFP "To Develop and Operate Transitional and Permanent Supportive Housing Facilities in the City of San Diego for Homeless Adults with Serious Mental Illness or Dual Diagnosis" invited qualified housing developers, nonprofit organizations, property owners, and development teams to submit proposals to create more supportive housing, representing a key strategic initiative for achieving the goals of creating 100 new transitional and 100 new permanent supportive housing units in the next several years. As a result, providers only have to submit one grant response to access all the above sources of money, making it easier and less costly to write proposals. Respondents felt that this blended approach was the best way to get proposals for programs that meet their requirements for ending chronic street homelessness, and anticipate repeating the process as funding permits. In the end the joint RFP was able to fund additional transitional units through Vietnam Veterans of San Diego, but did not result in the development of any additional permanent supportive housing units. However, the RFP did provide a model for future collaborative housing projects.

Stable Funnel Mechanisms. Both Columbus and Philadelphia have stable funnel mechanisms to make providers' lives easier.

Columbus

Rebuilding Lives is Columbus' integrated approach for moving chronically street homeless people to housing. As described in Chapter 4, resources for Rebuilding Lives are managed by a specially created "Funder Collaborative" that helps funders meet mutual goals as well as smoothing resource acquisition for providers. Members of the Funder Collaborative include the Community Shelter Board (which oversees the implementation of Rebuilding Lives, chairs the Funder Collaborative, and serves as the main fiscal agent for the initiative), the Alcohol, Drug, and Mental Health Board of Franklin County (ADAMH), City of Columbus Administration, Columbus City Council, Columbus Foundation, Columbus Health Department, Columbus Mayor's Office, Columbus Medical Association Foundation, Columbus Metropolitan Housing Authority, Corporation for Supportive Housing, Franklin County Department of Job & Family Services, Franklin County MR/DD, Franklin County Administration, Franklin County Office on Aging, Mid-Ohio Regional Planning Commission, Ohio Capital Corporation for Housing, United Way of Central Ohio, and the Veterans' Service Commission. Since Rebuilding Lives was launched, the Funder Collaborative has met monthly and now meets every other month to address funding and system issues—serving as the main mechanism for coordinating and monitoring the system.

Providers apply to CSB for a whole project, indicating the types of services and housing for which they need funding. CSB funds a project as a whole, funneling the money it receives from the sources described above in response to provider proposals and specifying reporting requirements. Projects may also receive direct funding through HUD's Supportive Housing Program, a small share of state dollars, and other funds. For the current year, the Rebuilding Lives budget is $5 million, most of which is for permanent supportive housing. Major funders are the Franklin County Board of Commissioners, the City of Columbus, and the United Way of Central Ohio.

CSB does not fund capital grants but it does help agencies secure such grants. Now that it has a better sense of the actual costs of permanent supportive housing, it is better able to predict the financial needs of a project (and operational and service costs have to be renewable). The costs are about $14,000 per unit per year for operations (mostly rent) and services.

HUD dollars are the primary Federal dollars used to support Rebuilding Lives. There are no real restrictions on them other than to use them for supportive housing; "they are flexible and we can use them well" says CSB's director. There are some challenges associated with Federal guidelines passed within the last several years, such as tenants not having any prior felony convictions; CSB is still working on resolving these kinds of barriers to housing. Although each PHA uses the same Federal guidelines, they are just guidelines and each PHA can choose whether to embrace, weaken, strength, or enforce those guidelines.

Philadelphia

In Philadelphia, staff members at city offices combine local money with Federal and state money to address the needs of chronically street homeless individuals. Homeless assistance programs fall primarily under the responsibility of the city's Offices of Housing and Community Development and Adult Services (OHCD and AS). OHCD receives ESG, CDBG, HOPWA, and other Federal resources, and conducts the annual Consolidated Plan process. It funds some transitional housing directly, and transfers Federal resources to AS for funding emergency shelter and additional transitional housing. City, state (Homeless Assistance Program), and Federal funds flow through AS and its component parts, the Office of Emergency Shelter and Services, the newly created Housing Support Center, Riverview Home (a city-owned personal care residence for elderly and/or vulnerable Philadelphians) and the Office of HIV Planning (a body responsible for coordinated planning for Federal funding from the Centers for Disease Control and Ryan White Title I). AS is also the City's convener for the annual Continuum of Care application. Some other agencies—Office of Mental Health, the Coordinating Office of Drug and Alcohol Abuse Programs, and the Department of Human Services (the child welfare office)—maintain small numbers of units that are closer to "housing plus services" than to treatment, and which accept homeless people as residents.

Philadelphia also combined the resources of social services with housing monies to create a stock of permanent supportive housing before homeless-specific Federal funding was available. In the early 1990s, the director of OHCD committed his agency to supplying housing in cases where the social services side of city government could and did supply the supportive services. At that time, Philadelphia had underspent its CDBG allotment for a number of years, so that money was made available to support transitional and permanent housing development.

Agencies As Funding Funnels to Ease Client Access to Services

As difficult as it is for agencies to assemble adequate funding to cover all their offerings, homeless people themselves often have an equally or more difficult time putting together the care they need. Conflicting eligibility criteria, lengthy application procedures, dispersed service locations, and simple ignorance about options and opportunities often mean that chronically homeless people do not get the services and supports that could help them leave homelessness.

"Case management," (which may mean a variety of things in different contexts) is often expected to help clients overcome these obstacles to getting appropriate services, and often it does just that. Case managers in most communities use their skills to broker the disparate services and programs that may be involved in aiding an individual homeless person. In our site visits we encountered some examples of "next steps" beyond simple case management that had decided advantages for clients—programs that within themselves combine enough varieties of funding, to cover enough varieties of supports, that they can "do whatever it takes" to help the client. They also had the accounting and fiscal sophistication to bill the appropriate funding sources without the client having to worry about eligibility. We found two forms of "funnel mechanisms" at the client level—mini-continuums and non-residential wraparound programs.

Mini-continuums. Mini-continuums bear mention here for their particular approach to funneling support to clients. The umbrella agency for a mini-continuum takes pains to acquire funding from many sources so that regardless of client characteristics every client is able to receive all the services offered. Clients are usually unaware of the funding sources for the services they receive. They may know that the agency is trying to help them obtain SSI, or Medicaid, or transitional cash benefits, but they also know that they will receive services whether or not they end up qualifying for these programs. Agency staff members offer clients whatever services they need, and then determine how to report service numbers and bill their funders. For example, the Lamp Community in Los Angeles receives a certain amount of AB 2034 money to serve clients coming from jail. However, the program continues to serve these clients once they have reached the "capacity" allowed under AB 2034 funds. All clients in the Lamp Community are offered available services as needed. Other examples of agencies that blend funding streams to serve clients comprehensively are Pine Street Inn and Friends of Shattuck Shelter in Boston, and several mini-continuums in Seattle.

A final example is Birmingham Health Care (BHC), which we highlight because it is quite unusual to find a full mini-continuum growing out of a program that began as a Health Care for the Homeless site. BHC's continuum begins with prevention, as its health clinics serve low-income communities generally, as well as homeless people. All people using BHC clinics are screened for housing needs, and referrals are made as needed. BHC has emergency shelter capacity in the form of hotel/motel vouchers, and also operates transitional and permanent supportive housing programs. Its fully certified health provider status means it has the ability to offer, and integrate, health, mental health, substance abuse, HIV/AIDS, and housing programs and services. BHC maintains one integrated client file across all programs and services, reinforcing to its employees the message that they are to consider, and work with, the whole person regardless of the "presenting problem."

"Whatever it takes" case management. Two of San Diego's most important programs focused on chronic street homeless people use an interesting approach to delivering supportive services to keep people in housing—they contract with behavioral health companies, one for-profit and one nonprofit. REACH contracts with Telecare Corporation for mental health case management, while Mental Health Systems, Inc. provides assessment, case management, and substance abuse and mental health services for SIP participants. REACH Program participants may also access other providers for a variety of services through their case manager. These companies are able to deliver appropriate care with workers who often are dual-certified for mental health and substance abuse treatment and have experience with people coming from corrections settings. They are also sophisticated enough to handle Medicaid claims (Medi-Cal in California), and are able to finance a significant portion of the services they provide through Medi-Cal billing, after helping clients qualify for SSI and Medi-Cal. The more Medi-Cal pays for the services it will cover, the more program service dollars can be devoted to other service needs. These companies also have county contracts for health, mental health, and substance abuse care, and thus are able to serve clients as needed and bill whichever source will pay, without troubling the clients about multiple program eligibility rules, applications, and so on. In addition to these advantages of contracted behavioral health services, the REACH program has succeeded in increasing to 85 percent (from about 15 percent) the people receiving cash and other public benefits (usually health insurance, food stamps, SSI, and other cash assistance). As with expanded Medicaid billing, increased client receipt of public benefits increases the overall resources available to help them remain stably housed.

For this approach to work, clients must have housing from another source, as they do in San Diego. The case management agencies must also have multiple sources of funding, including some that will let them serve indigents without other insurance. In the San Diego case both agencies have service contracts with the county Mental Health Services agency to provide mental health and substance abuse services. While these case management agencies do connect clients to specialty services outside their areas of expertise when needed (e.g., to job readiness and training opportunities), they are able to supply the core health, mental health, and substance abuse services within their own framework and in partnership with the clients' housing providers.

Potentially Underused Funding Opportunities

The Ohio program office of the Corporation for Supportive Housing assembled a list of funding sources that she felt were underused in Columbus (Community Shelter Board, 2003). Columbus *does* use some of these, as do others of the communities we visited. As the list is likely to be interesting to many readers, we reproduce it here as Table 6.2; we have added a few potential sources, which appear in *italics*. The list includes state and local as well as Federal sources. To the extent that a state and community does not have particular types of funding, the list may also serve as a source of ideas for stimulating the creation of new state and local funding sources.

Finding the resources to pay for new programs and services is always a challenge. The experience of these seven communities indicates very strongly that reducing chronic street homelessness requires significant investment of mainstream public agencies, bringing both their commitment and energy, and *local* dollars. The goal cannot be met if the homeless assistance network providers are the only players, and Federal funding streams the only resources.

Communities are probably most familiar with the traditional Federal sources of funding for homeless-related activities, but as this chapter shows, more Federal sources exist than some may think. Perhaps even more important for many readers are the different funding sources that some state or local jurisdictions have developed to address chronic homelessness. These include a housing tax levy (Seattle), tax increment financing generated by a redevelopment agency and reinvested in permanent supportive housing (San Diego), community redevelopment bonds.

(Philadelphia), special state funding streams (California's Integrated Services for Homeless People with Mental Illness, and its Supportive Housing Initiative Act), and investments by Business Improvement Districts and other associations of downtown businesses and corporations (Birmingham, Columbus, Philadelphia, San Diego). Philadelphia's Community Behavioral Health also provides a unique source of public funding for homeless services. Part of its structure to insurers, including Medicaid, that help pay for services is a "profit" margin. As a city agency, it is committed to investing a part of this "profit" margin into homeless assistance services such as outreach that are not reimbursable on a fee-for-services basis, and in housing. Other states and localities may be more willing to replicate these funding sources once policy makers have evidence that making certain types of investment in ending chronic street homelessness pays off in savings in other areas.

Table 6.2: Potentially Underused Funding Sources For Ending Chronic Street Homelessness

Capital Sources

- Department of Veterans Affairs – Capital grants for Veterans projects.
- Federal Home Loan Bank – Affordable housing development grants.
- HUD Section 811 – Use is for disabled, very low income; has experienced significant funding cutbacks in recent years.
- HUD Section 202 – Use is for seniors, very low income.
- *Community Development Block Grant—states have flexibility to use for capital needs.*
- State Housing Trust Fund – Gap funding for affordable housing projects.
- City/County Housing Trust Fund – Bridge loans for affordable housing projects.
- State Bond Funds – Long-term financing.
- *State or Local Housing Finance Agency—long-term, low-interest financing.*
- State General Funds – Ohio Department of Mental Health grants for mentally disabled housing development.

Sources for Supportive Housing Operating Costs

- State General Funds – Ohio Department of Mental Health and Ohio Department of Alcohol and Drug Addiction Services grants for operating.
- State Housing Trust Fund – Operating grants for affordable housing (<35% area median income).
- HUD HOPWA (Housing Opportunities for People with AIDS) – Operating grants for AIDS/HIV.
- HUD Section 202 – Provides rental subsidies through 5-year contracts.

Table 6.2 – Continued

- HUD Section 811 – Provides rental subsidies through 5-year contracts; program has had major cutbacks.
- Capitalized Reserves – Legal agreements needed; source of funds are Low Income Housing Tax Credit investment proceeds, Community Development Block Grant, HUD Section 811, Housing Trust Funds or other local General Revenue which are not statutorily or legally prohibited.
- Special state-funded supportive housing demonstrations – Have been successful in other states like Michigan, Minnesota, Illinois, and Connecticut.

Sources for Services
- HUD HOPWA (Housing Opportunities for People with AIDS) – Provides services for people with AIDS/HIV.
- Federal SAMHSA (Substance Abuse & Mental Health Services Administration) – programmatic grants.
- Federal PATH (Projects for Assistance in Transition from Homelessness) – Provides services for people with mental illness.
- "System of Care" models have been successful in Indianapolis, Minnesota and California.
- Medicaid and Medicaid Waiver programs, *including Medical Rehabilitation Option* – A local Medicaid Work Group continues to evaluate how best to use this as a source.
- SSI/SSDI – Payments, when appropriate, can be paid directly to the housing or service provider; can offset the cost of services.
- *Federal Block Grants—Social Services, Mental Health, Substance Abuse, Preventive Health, Community Services – States have flexibility to determine services delivered, eligibility, and distribution method.*
- Federal, state & county criminal justice systems – Have been successful in Illinois and New York.
- Special state funded supportive housing demonstrations – Have been successful in other states.
- State Housing Trust Funds – Could be a resource if OHTF has stable and growing source of revenue.

POLICY, PRACTICE, AND
RESEARCH IMPLICATIONS

This is a time when communities are exploring new approaches to end chronic street homelessness. Realistically, the approaches are still at the stage of reducing such homelessness, and the evaluations of their success are still rudimentary. We selected seven communities that were reputed to have made progress in reducing their chronic street homeless population and would be able to document that progress. After conducting site visits, we found that only three of the seven had developed a true community-wide paradigm, but that each of the seven communities had made noteworthy innovations at the strategic level. Our research suggests that certain elements are essential for a community to make significant progress toward the goal of ending homelessness.

Above all our study indicates that reducing, and eventually ending, chronic homelessness is an achievable goal that will require permanent supportive housing programs. Moreover success will require a clear recognition of this goal, community-wide collaboration, strong leadership within an effective organizational structure, and significant resources from mainstream public agencies. Other elements that will increase the likelihood of success are significant resources from the private sector, commitment and support from elected officials, outcome evaluation mechanisms for program support and improvement, openness to new service approaches, and strategies to minimize negative neighborhood reactions to projects. In this chapter we explore the implications of these findings.

Implications for Policy

Our study has found that the most successful communities were employing community-wide, integrated approaches to reduce chronic homelessness. However, such approaches were not widespread. We searched for communities meeting these criteria and only found three. The scarcity of exemplary sites suggests that the effectiveness of community-wide, integrated approaches needs to be publicized. Communities also need assistance in recognizing and implementing the elements necessary for success, and funding support from Federal, state, and local agencies that is directed toward these new strategies.

During site visits many respondents offered suggestions for how Federal policy and Federal agencies could help them as they pursue their goal of ending chronic homelessness. Their suggestions reflect their own experiences of what has helped them, and also what they feel could continue to ease the way toward reaching their goal. These include suggestions for Federal, state, and local agencies. A particular problem for communities was that diverse, uncoordinated funding streams required them to submit numerous proposals to many different agencies in order to provide total wraparound housing and supportive services for the chronically homeless. The policy implications of these findings are:

- Federal agencies should continue to prioritize community-wide planning and integrated approaches for reducing chronic homelessness in general, and street homelessness for people with severe mental illness, chronic substance abuse, HIV/AIDS, or any combination in particular.
- Federal agencies should make technical assistance widely available to teams from communities that have reached the stage of starting to plan an approach to reducing street homelessness.
- Federal agencies should facilitate opportunities for practitioners and planners to observe new approaches in action, speak with consumers, see results, and consider how these practices could be applied in their own community.
- Federal legislative action should increase the flexibility of Federal agencies to blend their funding to support innovative community-wide practices that integrate services across local agencies to reduce chronic homelessness. State and local agencies should adjust rules and regulations to facilitate access to mainstream benefits, programs, and services for chronically street homeless people.
- State and local agencies should establish procedures and resources to assure that people leaving psychiatric care, substance abuse treatment, correctional facilities, or foster care do not become homeless.
- State and local agencies should facilitate capacity to serve chronically homeless clients by improving liaison and integrated service arrangements among mental health, substance abuse, medical care, and housing authorities.

Implications for Practice

The site appendices of this report include "practices of potential interest to other communities" with contact information for people who are involved in these activities. Readers should browse these practices to see whether any of them might be appropriate for their own community. There are, however, some general implications for practice. To successfully reduce chronic homelessness within a community:

- Homeless providers need to develop dual competence and dual certification—mental illness and substance abuse issues must be handled together.
- Mainstream mental health and substance abuse agencies need to have an integrated approach to mental illness and substance abuse for chronically street homeless people.
- Mainstream health, mental health, substance abuse, and welfare agencies should make their clients' housing stability a high priority and create positions of housing developers and coordinators.
- Housing providers need to understand the benefits of supportive services to their *whole* tenant base and not just to those who were once homeless.
- Strong, skilled leaders committed to an integrated community-wide approach need to come forward and have the backing and resources of local mainstream agencies and elected officials.

Implications for Research

Although the study communities were documenting the "success" of their approaches, research on the outcomes and the cost effectiveness of their various strategies often had flaws in design or incomplete data. We discovered many gaps in knowledge that hindered our ability to establish with greater confidence which approaches and strategies were most fruitful and hold the most promise for other communities. The following research suggestions are those that we think will provide the most useful information to show effective approaches to ending chronic street homelessness.

- Longitudinal tracking studies should follow people once they leave supported housing to document housing stability. A primary outcome to observe in this research would be housing stability within and after leaving the homeless assistance network, and what factors contribute to it. These studies would be most relevant to conduct for formerly street homeless people with severe mental illness and co-occurring disorders.

- Research should compare the effectiveness and cost-effectiveness of different pathways into permanent housing for different subpopulations. Ideally this research would use random assignment intervention studies; if that is impossible, it *must* employ meaningful comparison groups.

- Research on pathways should include (1) directly from the street into permanent supportive housing, (2) directly from the street into transitional housing as a step before permanent supportive housing, (3) directly from the street into safe haven as a step before permanent supportive housing, and (4) transitional housing with expectation of movement into affordable housing in the community (no supportive services).

- Research should test the following approaches within the pathways just described (1) sober versus harm reduction models, (2) voluntary versus coerced treatment (the latter through drug court or its equivalent), (3) different physical structures and service delivery mechanisms (for example, scattered site, only-formerly-homeless single site, and mixed-use single site), and (4) if transitional housing is part of the pathway being tested, what is the optimal duration of transitional housing to increase the odds of maintaining recovery.

- Research should support a reasonable sample of permanent supportive housing providers to collect and maintain better data on their tenants, and assemble these data at the national level. The providers would need to collect data (1) at intake about tenant histories, (2) during residence, and (3) after people leave permanent supportive housing, to document continued progress or return to homelessness. To give this approach the greatest chance to contribute high quality information, a national research effort would have to be established to manage data collection within programs and conduct the follow-up interviewing, if one wanted to assure acceptable completion levels.

REFERENCES

Andersen, A., LLP; Center for Mental Health Policy and Services Research, University of Pennsylvania; K. E. Sherwood; and TWP Consulting. 2000. *Connecticut Supportive Housing Demonstration Program: Final Program Evaluation Report,* New Haven, CT: Corporation for Supportive Housing.

Boston Foundation. 2002. *Boston Indicators Report 2002.* Boston, MA: Author.

Burt, M. R., D. Pollack, A. Sosland, K. S. Mikelson, E. Drapa, K. Greenwalt, and P. Sharkey, 2002. *Evaluation of Continuums of Care for Homeless People: Final Report.* Prepared for U.S. Department of Housing and Urban Development. Washington, D.C.: U.S. Government Printing Office.

Campbell, M. 2001. "Lack of Affordable Housing a Detriment to City," *Birmingham Business Journal,* 30 April.

City of Boston. 2000. Leading the Way: A Report on Boston's Housing Strategy FY 2001-2003. Boston, MA: Author.

City of Philadelphia. 1996. Five Year Financial Plan: Fiscal Year 1997-Fiscal Year 2001. Philadelphia, PA: Author.

Coalition on Homelessness and Housing in Ohio. 1999. "Homelessness a 'Major Community Issue' for Central Ohioans," *Breaking Ground,* December: 1-6.

Community Research Partners. 2001. How We are Doing in Central Ohio: Areas of Progress and Areas of Concern. Columbus, OH: Author.

Community Shelter Board. 2003. Moving Forward, March 2003, *Rebuilding Lives: Breaking the Cycle of Homelessness.* Columbus, OH: Author.

——. 2003. "Executive Summary, Stakeholder's Input to FY 2003 Allocation Recommendations and Application Process: Report to the Board of Trustees, January 30, 2003," Columbus, OH.: Author.

——. 2002. Preventing Homelessness: *Discharge Planning from Corrections Facilities.* Columbus, OH: Author.

——. 2001. "Ending Homelessness in Columbus," Briefing for Members of the U.S. House of Representatives, Financial Services Committee, and the U.S. Department of Housing and Urban Development, November. Columbus, OH: Author.

——. 1999. Good Neighbor and Shelter Certification: Draft for Public Comment, 30 November. Columbus, OH: Author.

Corporation for Supportive Housing. 2001. *California Supportive Housing Resource Guide: FY 2001/2002.* Oakland, CA: Author.

Culhane, D. P., E. F. Dejowski, J. Ibanez, E. Needham, and I. Macchia. 1994. "Public Shelter Admission Rates in Philadelphia and New York City: Implications for Sheltered Population Counts," *Housing Policy Debate,* 5(2): 107-163.

Culhane, D. P. and R. Kuhn. 1998. "Patterns and Determinants of Public Shelter Utilization Among Homeless Adults in New York City and Philadelphia" *Journal of Policy Analysis and Management,* 17(1): 23-43.

Culhane, D. P., S. Metraux, and T. Hadley. 2002. "Public Service Reductions Associated with Placement of Homeless Persons with Severe Mental Illness in Supportive Housing," *Housing Policy Debate,* 13(1): 107-163.

Davis, G., G. Johnson, and S.W. Mayberg. 2003. *Effectiveness of Integrated Services for Homeless Adults with Serious Mental Illness*: A Report to the Legislature as Required by Division 5, Section 5814, of California Welfare and Institutions Code. Sacramento, CA: California Department of Mental Health.

——— 2002. Effectiveness of Integrated Services for Homeless Adults with Serious Mental Illness: A Report to the Legislature as Required by Division 5, Section 5814, of California Welfare and Institutions Code. Sacramento, CA: California Department of Mental Health.

Emergency Shelter Commission. 2002. Homelessness *in the City of Boston Winter 2002-2003*: Annual Census Report. Boston, MA: Author.

Goldstein, H. 1990. *Problem-Oriented Policing.* New York, NY: McGraw-Hill.

Grieff, D., T. Proscio, and C. Wilkins. 2003. *Laying a New Foundation: Changing the Systems that Create and Sustain Supportive Housing.* New York, NY: Corporation for Supportive Housing.

Greater Philadelphia Urban Affairs Coalition, 1998. *Our Way Home: A Blueprint to End Homelessness in Philadelphia.* Philadelphia, PA: Author.

Hiller, A. and D. Culhane. 2003. *Closing the Gap*: Housing (un)Affordability in Philadelphia.

Philadelphia, PA: Cartographic Modeling Laboratory, University of Pennsylvania.

Hunter, I., A. Sheff, B. Roth, and A. Dinova. 2002. *Welcome to...AB34/AB 2034:*

Comprehensive, *Community-based Treatment Services for the Homeless, Forensic Mentally Ill.* San Fernando Valley, CA: San Fernando Valley Community Mental Health Center, Inc.

International Downtown Association. 2000. *Addressing Homelessness: Successful Downtown Partnerships.* Washington, D.C.: Author.

Kasprow, W. J., R. Rosenheck, D. DiLella, and L. Cavallaro. 2002. *Health Care for Homeless Veterans Programs: Fifteenth Annual Report.* West Haven, CT: Northeast Program Evaluation Center.

Kessler, K. and J. Wartell. 1996. "Community Law Enforcement: The Success of San Diego's Volunteer Policing Program." Los Angeles, CA: Los Angeles Reason Public Policy Institute.

Konrad, E. L. 1996. "A Multidimensional Framework for Conceptualizing Human Services for Integration Initiatives," *New Directions for Evaluation,* 69: 5-19.

Kromer, J. 2001. Neighborhood Recovery: Reinvestment Policy for the New Hometown. New Brunswick, NJ: Rutgers University Press.

Lamp Community. 2002. *The Philosophical Framework of the Community Model*: An Approach to Providing Comprehensive Housing and Services to Homeless Individuals with Chronic Mental Illness. Los Angeles, CA: Author.

Martinez, T. and M. R. Burt. 2003. *Changes in Service Use Patterns for Chronically Homeless People Placed in Permanent Supportive Housing.* Oakland, CA: Corporation for Supportive Housing.

McGuire, J., S. Berman, W. Daniels, A. N. Tran, and A. Mares. 2001. *Creating VA-Community Partnerships for Housing Homeless Veterans: The VA West Los Angeles Healthcare Center Experience.* Los Angeles, CA: Department of Veterans Affairs Greater Los Angeles Healthcare System.

Menino, T. M. 2002. *Leading the Wa*y: A Midpoint Progress Report on Boston's Housing Strategy FY 2001-2003. Boston, MA: City of Boston.

————. 2000. *Leading the Way: A Report on Boston's Housing Strategy* FY 2001-2003. Boston, MA: City of Boston.

Melaville, A. L. and M. J. Blank. 1991. *What It Takes: Structuring Interagency Partnerships to Connect Children and Families with Comprehensive Services.* Washington, D.C.: Education and Human Services Consortium.

National Alliance to End Homeless. 2000. *A Plan, Not A Dream: How to End Homelessness in Ten Years.* Washington, D.C.: Author.

Northwest Resource Associates. 2002. *Evaluation of the Lyon Building Supported Housing Program.* Seattle, WA: Northwest Resource Associates.

Office of Emergency Shelter and Services. 1997. *Fact Sheet.* Philadelphia, PA: City of Philadelphia.

———. 1996. *Year End Report.* Philadelphia, PA: City of Philadelphia.

O'Hara, A. and E. Cooper. 2003. *Priced Out in 2002.* Boston, MA: Technical Assistance Collaborative.

Orwin, R. G., H. H. Goldman, L.J. Sonnefeld, M. S. Ridgely, N. G. Smith, R. Garrison-Mogren, E. O'Neill and A. Sherman. 1994. "Alcohol And Drug Abuse Treatment of Homeless Persons: Results from the NIAAA Community Demonstration Program," *Journal of Health Care for the Poor and Underserved,* 5 (4): 326-352.

Proscio, Tony. 2000. Supportive Housing and Its Impact on the Public Health Crisis of Homelessness, New York, NY: Corporation for Supportive Housing.

Rosenheck, Robert, W. Kasprow, L. Frisman, and W. Liu-Mares. 2003. "Cost-effectiveness of Supportive Housing for Homeless Persons with Mental Illness," *Archives of General Psychiatry,* 60 (September): 940-951.

Rosenheck, R., W. Kasprow, L. Frisman, and L. Wen. (n.d.) *An Experimental Study of Supported Housing for Homeless Persons with Mental Illness.* West Haven, CT: Northeast Program Evaluation Center.

Seattle/King County Coalition for the Homeless. 2003. The 24th Annual One Night Count of People Who Are Homeless in King County, Washington. Seattle, WA: Author.

Shern, D.L., C. J. Felton, R. L. Hough, A. F. Lehman, S. M. Goldfinger, E. Valencia, D. Dennis, R. Straw and P. A. Wood. 1997. "Housing Outcomes for Homeless Adults with Mental Illness: Results from the Second-Round McKinney Program," *Psychiatric Services,* 48 (2): 239–241.

Strategic Homeless Planning Group. 2000. *Boston Strategic Homeless Planning Group: Summary Report.* Boston, Massachusetts: Author.

Tsemberis, S. and R. F. Eisenberg. 2000. "Pathways to Housing: Supported Housing for Street-Dwelling Homeless Individuals with Psychiatric Disabilities," *Psychiatric Services,* 51 (4): 487-493.

Urban Land Institute. 2002 Downtown Birmingham, Alabama: A Master-Planning Process for Downtown, Washington, D.C.: Author.

U.S. Department of Housing and Urban Development. 2002. "Fair Market Rents for the Housing Choice Voucher Program and Moderate Rehabilitation Single Room Occupancy Program Fiscal Year 2003," *Federal Register Part II,* 30 September: 4.

———. 1995. *National Evaluation of the Supportive Housing Demonstration Program.* Washington, D.C.: U.S. Government Printing Office.

INDEX

A

acceptance, 61
access, 3, 4, 6, 8, 11, 23, 44, 46, 51, 54,
    55, 56, 58, 59, 67, 68, 72, 73, 74, 76,
    77, 79, 83, 89, 106, 116, 120, 125
accommodation, 1, 2, 61
accountability, 87
accounting, 119
accuracy, 35
achievement, 63, 87
addiction, 75, 79, 103
adjustment, 9
adults, 14, 33, 97, 99, 110
advocacy, 38, 51, 75, 81, 83, 86, 88
affect, 62, 67
age, 4, 10, 96, 110
agent, 7, 117
aggregation, 45
AIDS, 66, 122, 123
alcohol, 5, 34, 54, 66, 84, 88, 108
alcohol problems, 5
alcoholics, 57
alternative(s), 48, 57, 78, 81, 82, 94, 104,
    115
appendix, 40
arrest, 57
assault, 13
assessment, 18, 57, 74, 101, 120
assignment, 104

association, 46, 91
attention, 5, 43, 52, 83, 93, 104, 113
Attorney General, 13
attractiveness, 79
authority, 36, 39, 43, 46, 56, 66, 86, 108,
    116
autonomy, 60
availability, 10, 12, 79
averaging, 56
avoidance, 10, 103

B

banks, 7
barriers, 34, 59, 76, 77, 87, 88, 89, 117
behavior, 64, 81
birth, 6
body, 15, 33, 61, 88, 118
bonds, 108, 109, 122
breakdown, 27
breakfast, 78
buildings, 15, 16, 18, 39, 66, 67, 89, 97,
    109

C

campaigns, 83
candidates, 83
CAP, 48

career development, 36
census, 3, 129
child development, 11
childhood, 5
children, 4, 6, 7, 8, 11, 14, 23, 77, 97, 112
circulation, 20
classes, 77
clients, 4, 39, 44, 47, 58, 59, 61, 62, 69, 70, 72, 73, 74, 75, 76, 77, 78, 79, 80, 98, 99, 101, 104, 105, 106, 110, 113, 115, 118, 119, 120, 125
closure, 92
collaboration, 43, 44, 57, 71, 80, 124
combined effect, 52
commitment, 22, 34, 35, 44, 49, 53, 55, 68, 79, 80, 83, 85, 87, 88, 91, 98, 121, 124
communication, 43, 44, 52, 66, 71, 80, 89
community, 8, 9, 10, 12, 14, 15, 17, 18, 19, 20, 21, 24, 32, 33, 34, 35, 36, 37, 39, 40, 41, 42, 43, 44, 45, 47, 48, 49, 51, 52, 53, 57, 58, 62, 63, 65, 66, 67, 69, 70, 79, 80, 81, 82, 83, 84, 85, 86, 87, 89, 90, 91, 92, 93, 94, 95, 96, 105, 108, 110, 113, 121, 124, 125, 126, 127
community relations, 51, 52, 91
community service, 36, 65, 67
community support, 18, 83, 85
competence, 126
complexity, 35, 103
compliance, 52, 57
components, 9, 10, 18, 35, 40, 54, 78, 79
conduct, 3, 34, 42, 52, 57, 63, 74, 127
confidence, 55, 126
confidentiality, 68
conflict of interest, 67
consciousness, 103
consensus, 2
consolidation, 17, 24
construction, 49, 109, 112
consumers, 56, 100, 103, 115, 125

context, 46, 57
control, 36, 51, 54, 60, 64, 92
conversion, 16, 111
corporations, 38, 121
cost effectiveness, 50, 126
cost saving, 110
costs, 16, 18, 50, 61, 68, 90, 92, 98, 102, 103, 104, 105, 106, 107, 108, 110, 117
counseling, 10, 11, 12, 18, 20, 21
coverage, 93
covering, 77
CPC, 75, 97
credit, 11

D

damage, 78
data collection, 127
data set, 4
database, 55, 56, 70, 71, 72, 73, 75, 80, 91
death, 5
decisions, 10, 66, 87
definition, 1, 2, 22
delivery, 37, 38, 44, 51, 66, 70, 127
delusions, 74
demand, 3, 38, 42, 55, 61, 62, 63, 64, 67, 79, 82, 111
demographics, 4
Department of Health and Human Services, 8, 12, 25, 28
Department of Homeland Security, 7
Department of Justice, 12, 13, 24
Department of the Interior, 6
direct measure, 93
disabilities, 14, 23, 34, 51, 53, 58, 59, 96, 97, 98, 99, 103, 108, 110, 115
disability, 64
disorder, 20
displacement, 49, 86
distribution, 5, 21, 67, 123
division, 67
division of labor, 67

domestic violence, 4, 12, 13
donations, 49, 109
donors, 84
downsizing, 89
drug abuse, 16, 34, 66
drug addict, 84, 108
drug addiction, 84, 108
drug treatment, 88
drug use, 63
drugs, 54, 62
duplication, 71, 75
duration, 4, 127

E

economic activity, 108
economic development, 47
elderly, 18, 108, 118
election, 83
employees, 25, 120
employment, 12, 14, 16, 18, 19, 20, 23,
    24, 36, 48, 65, 66, 89, 115
enrollment, 6, 104, 110
environment, 55
epidemic, 96
ethnicity, 96
evidence, 35, 79, 92, 103, 122
expectation, 127
expenditures, 103, 104, 107
expertise, 20, 56, 120
experts, 21
exploitation, 11

F

faith, 5, 10, 16, 18, 83
family, 2, 10, 16, 53, 58, 62, 73, 78, 96,
    99, 101
family members, 58, 78
federal funds, 8
feedback, 44
FEMA, 7, 26, 114
finance, 106, 108, 113, 120

financial resources, 84
financing, 107, 108, 109, 111, 121, 122
flexibility, 23, 78, 122, 123, 125
focus groups, 35, 64
focusing, 73
food, 3, 5, 6, 7, 14, 21, 48, 120
free choice, 68
friends, 2, 68, 73, 101
fuel, 105
funding, 8, 9, 11, 12, 13, 15, 16, 18, 20,
    24, 25, 27, 28, 34, 36, 37, 39, 40, 46,
    48, 50, 67, 80, 81, 82, 83, 84, 90, 106,
    107, 109, 110, 111, 112, 113, 115,
    116, 117, 118, 119, 120, 121, 122,
    124, 125
fundraising, 48

G

GI Bill, 25
goals, 10, 19, 33, 42, 44, 53, 80, 85, 88,
    91, 116
government, 5, 10, 16, 17, 21, 36, 39, 45,
    83, 85, 86, 90, 91, 115, 118
grants, 6, 7, 8, 9, 10, 11, 12, 13, 14, 15,
    16, 18, 20, 23, 48, 110, 112, 116, 117,
    122, 123
groups, 10, 11, 20, 79, 91, 127
growth, 47
guidance, 3, 5, 11, 37
guidelines, 7, 20, 40, 90, 93, 117

H

harm, 51, 63, 64, 65, 79, 127
health, 5, 6, 7, 8, 11, 14, 16, 17, 18, 21,
    23, 25, 38, 42, 46, 47, 50, 55, 56, 57,
    61, 63, 66, 68, 71, 75, 77, 89, 90, 91,
    92, 96, 98, 108, 119, 120, 126
health care, 18, 23, 25, 66, 77, 89, 108
health insurance, 120
health services, 6, 8, 14, 76, 89, 120
high school, 4

hip, 85
HIV, 34, 37, 53, 118, 119, 122, 123, 125
HIV/AIDS, 34, 37, 53, 119, 125
home care services, 18
home ownership, 108
hospitalization, 104, 110
host, 10
housing, 2, 4, 5, 8, 12, 13, 14, 15, 17, 18, 19, 20, 22, 23, 24, 25, 31, 32, 33, 36, 37, 38, 39, 42, 43, 47, 49, 50, 51, 52, 53, 54, 55, 56, 57, 58, 59, 60, 61, 62, 63, 64, 66, 67, 68, 69, 70, 72, 73, 74, 75, 77, 78, 79, 81, 82, 83, 84, 85, 86, 87, 88, 89, 90, 91, 92, 93, 94, 95, 96, 97, 98, 99, 100, 101, 102, 103, 104, 105, 106, 107, 108, 109, 110, 111, 112, 113, 114, 115, 116, 117, 118, 119, 120, 121, 122, 123, 124, 125, 126, 127

I

ideas, 87, 121
illegal drug use, 64
immunization, 6
implementation, 34, 84, 117
in transition, 21
incarceration, 58, 78, 104, 110
incentives, 115
income, 15, 16, 23, 39, 52, 60, 66, 83, 89, 96, 98, 107, 108, 110, 111, 119, 122
income support, 23, 66
independence, 11
influence, 92
inmates, 58, 76, 78
institutions, 10, 21, 32, 54, 69, 70, 76
instruction, 66
insurance, 16, 106, 120
integration, 21, 60, 90
intensity, 21, 71, 101
interaction, 12, 71
interactions, 58, 80
interest, 33, 40, 78, 80, 111, 122, 126

interest rates, 111
interface, 69
intervention, 65, 127
intervention strategies, 65
investment, 34, 38, 80, 121, 122, 123

J

job skills, 77
job training, 109
jobs, 4, 65, 82, 115
jurisdiction, 7, 108
justice, 10, 123

K

knowledge, 44, 51, 80, 126

L

labor, 16
labor force, 16
land, 19, 47, 107
law enforcement, 10, 39, 50, 57, 65, 103
laws, 60
layoffs, 96
lead, 32, 36, 39, 46, 89
leadership, 33, 41, 45, 46, 48, 53, 80, 87, 88, 89, 91, 124
legislation, 5, 24, 25, 81
likelihood, 74, 124
linkage, 61
links, 46, 70, 75
literacy, 18
living environment, 60
loans, 20, 25, 78, 111, 113, 122
local community, 10
local government, 5, 7, 13, 14, 15, 16, 17, 22, 36
location, 70, 73, 76
locus, 98
logging, 71

M

major cities, 22
management, 8, 11, 12, 14, 18, 23, 25, 38, 50, 55, 64, 66, 67, 68, 69, 72, 73, 75, 77, 82, 92, 104, 107, 118, 120
mandates, 9
market, 39, 97, 115
mass, 7
meals, 18
measures, 68, 93, 105, 108
media, vii, 81
median, 122
Medicaid, 68, 71, 78, 114, 119, 120, 121, 123
Medicare, 113, 114
membership, 36
men, 4, 58, 77, 98, 102
mental health, 5, 8, 10, 14, 15, 17, 18, 23, 24, 25, 36, 38, 42, 46, 47, 50, 51, 55, 56, 57, 58, 61, 62, 66, 68, 69, 71, 74, 75, 76, 77, 78, 84, 90, 91, 92, 98, 99, 107, 108, 110, 119, 120, 125, 126
mental health professionals, 58
mental illness, 4, 20, 43, 51, 54, 57, 60, 80, 87, 96, 97, 98, 100, 109, 110, 126, 127
mergers, 51
Miami, 28
migration, 95
missions, 47
models, 59, 61, 62, 63, 103, 123, 127
momentum, 87
money, 11, 25, 36, 44, 50, 82, 92, 104, 107, 108, 109, 116, 117, 118, 119
monitoring, 50, 52, 117
mothers, 11
motivation, 67
movement, 47, 63, 89, 127
murder, 76
mutuality, 59

N

needs, 9, 18, 20, 22, 23, 24, 32, 34, 37, 39, 48, 49, 51, 54, 55, 56, 70, 73, 74, 78, 83, 84, 87, 88, 94, 95, 102, 108, 110, 111, 115, 117, 118, 124
negative consequences, 63
network, 8, 33, 36, 38, 39, 42, 47, 57, 72, 73, 74, 86, 89, 108, 113, 115, 121, 127
No Child Left Behind, 6
nursing, 18, 57

O

offenders, 35, 38, 57, 69
old age, 76
openness, 51, 53, 124
organization, 33, 36, 38, 41, 43, 44, 45, 53, 87, 89
organizational membership, 46
organizations, 7, 10, 12, 13, 14, 15, 16, 17, 18, 19, 21, 42, 46, 47, 49, 52, 79, 84, 89, 113, 116
orientation, 74
overload, 106
ownership, 109

P

Pacific, 97
paradigm shift, 33, 42, 43, 52, 53
parenting, 10, 11, 77
parole, 78
partnership, 38, 59, 78, 113, 121
pathways, 42, 127
peers, 87
permit, 64
personal control, 60
personal relationship, 77
personality, 45
persons with disabilities, 14
physical health, 11

planning, 36, 37, 39, 47, 48, 49, 50, 51, 54, 69, 70, 86, 93, 98, 118, 125
police, 39, 43, 56, 73, 78, 81, 82, 83, 86, 103, 107
policy makers, 122
political leaders, 85
politics, 88
poor, 36, 48, 77, 92
population, 1, 3, 4, 8, 10, 23, 32, 34, 38, 39, 44, 48, 49, 54, 57, 69, 71, 72, 76, 80, 82, 85, 88, 90, 91, 97, 98, 105, 106, 107, 108, 110, 112, 124
portfolio, 87
poverty, 3, 4, 111
power, 47, 52, 87
pressure, 81
prevention, 9, 16, 36, 51, 69, 70, 77, 119
prices, 97
principle, 60
prisons, 98
private investment, 111
private sector, 41, 46, 53, 106, 109, 124
problem-solving, 43, 86
production, 36, 108
profits, 5, 16
program, 2, 4, 5, 6, 8, 9, 10, 11, 12, 13, 14, 15, 16, 17, 18, 19, 20, 21, 24, 25, 27, 28, 35, 36, 37, 41, 42, 43, 44, 50, 53, 57, 58, 59, 60, 61, 62, 63, 64, 65, 66, 67, 68, 70, 72, 74, 75, 77, 78, 79, 85, 88, 89, 90, 93, 97, 98, 100, 101, 102, 103, 104, 107, 108, 110, 111, 112, 113, 116, 119, 120, 121, 123, 124
programming, 39
psychiatric institution, 69
public education, 6, 83
public health, 106
public housing, 4, 15, 46, 66, 107, 116
public policy, 37
public resources, 103, 107
public services, 23, 73, 103
public support, 81
Puerto Rico, 8

R

race, 4, 96
radio, 55
random assignment, 127
range, 21, 45, 48, 49, 63, 90
reality, 32, 53
recidivism, 50, 102
recidivism rate, 102
recognition, 31, 48, 124
recovery, 66, 79, 91, 127
recurrence, 115
redevelopment, 37, 39, 43, 47, 48, 86, 108, 109, 121
reduction, 16, 51, 61, 63, 64, 65, 79, 98, 105, 127
regulations, 125
rehabilitation, 15, 16, 18, 19, 21, 57, 77, 108, 111, 112
Rehabilitation Act, 19
rehabilitation program, 18, 19
relationship, 20, 59
relationships, 39, 51, 80, 85, 91
rent, 7, 15, 61, 62, 78, 79, 97, 100, 106, 110, 115, 117
rent subsidies, 15, 106, 110
repair, 78
resistance, 34, 60, 78, 89
resolution, 55, 86
resources, 8, 17, 22, 23, 24, 32, 33, 39, 41, 42, 44, 45, 46, 47, 48, 53, 55, 58, 68, 69, 73, 77, 79, 80, 81, 82, 83, 84, 85, 86, 87, 89, 91, 92, 96, 98, 102, 106, 107, 108, 109, 116, 118, 120, 121, 124, 125, 126
responsibility, 28, 69, 76, 77, 84, 118
retention, 59
returns, 96
revenue, 48, 84, 106, 108, 123
risk, 8, 10, 11, 15, 17, 25, 54, 58, 69, 110, 111

S

safety, 7, 21, 37, 48, 52, 84
Samoa, 6
sample, 3, 94, 95, 127
sample survey, 94, 95
savings, 50, 103, 104, 122
scarcity, 124
school, 4, 6, 7
search, 34
security, 21
self, 10, 20, 65, 67, 78, 98
self-esteem, 65
Senate, 24
sentencing, 78
separation, 10
series, 93
service provider, 7, 13, 32, 36, 39, 42,
    46, 59, 60, 62, 68, 69, 71, 73, 76, 84,
    89, 102, 115, 116, 123
services, 3, 4, 5, 6, 7, 8, 10, 11, 12, 13,
    14, 15, 16, 17, 18, 19, 20, 21, 23, 25,
    28, 32, 36, 37, 38, 39, 42, 44, 45, 46,
    48, 49, 50, 51, 54, 55, 56, 57, 58, 59,
    60, 61, 62, 64, 66, 67, 68, 70, 71, 72,
    73, 74, 75, 76, 77, 79, 80, 81, 82, 83,
    84, 85, 89, 90, 91, 92, 96, 97, 98, 100,
    101, 102, 103, 104, 105, 106, 107,
    108, 109, 110, 111, 112, 113, 114,
    115, 117, 118, 119, 120, 121, 123,
    125, 126, 127
sexual abuse, 11
shaping, 59
shelter, 1, 2, 3, 5, 10, 11, 12, 21, 22, 36,
    37, 38, 39, 43, 48, 49, 50, 51, 55, 56,
    59, 60, 61, 66, 69, 72, 77, 81, 83, 92,
    94, 95, 96, 97, 98, 101, 102, 111, 112,
    113, 115, 118, 119
sign, 73
sites, 7, 17, 35, 49, 51, 52, 61, 82, 111,
    124
skills, 11, 18, 23, 25, 53, 56, 66, 109,
    119
skills training, 18, 25

smoothing, 116
sobriety, 20, 42, 54, 61, 63, 65, 79
social events, 68
social services, 10, 15, 23, 24, 98, 118
spectrum, 39, 88
SSI, 60, 119, 120, 123
stability, 69, 74, 77, 87, 99, 126
stages, 52
stakeholders, 87
standards, 51, 78, 93
state mental hospitals, 92
statistics, 93, 104, 111
stimulant, 104
stock, 118
strategies, 13, 32, 33, 34, 39, 51, 53, 55,
    63, 64, 70, 78, 80, 83, 91, 124, 126
streams, 67, 106, 110, 112, 113, 115,
    119, 121, 125
strength, 86, 87, 117
stress, 52
students, 6
subsidy, 25
substance abuse, 4, 8, 15, 17, 20, 23, 24,
    25, 32, 36, 38, 42, 46, 47, 51, 53, 54,
    55, 57, 60, 61, 62, 63, 65, 68, 75, 76,
    77, 80, 82, 85, 96, 98, 99, 101, 103,
    108, 110, 115, 119, 120, 125, 126
substance addiction, 98
substance use, 21, 63, 64, 79
success rate, 107
suicidal ideation, 74
summer, 75
supply, 15, 58, 118, 120
surplus, 5, 38
survival, 53
symptoms, 54
systems, 10, 13, 23, 37, 38, 45, 50, 51,
    54, 67, 71, 77, 90, 123

T

tax credit, 111, 112
technical assistance, 9, 20, 38, 78, 79,
    125

technician, 56
technology, 70, 72, 80
telephone, 66
tenants, 14, 42, 59, 60, 61, 62, 66, 67, 68,
    79, 101, 111, 115, 117, 127
tension, 45, 81
terminally ill, 18
theory, 116
therapy, 19
time, 1, 7, 12, 16, 21, 23, 31, 32, 33, 39,
    51, 52, 53, 54, 58, 65, 75, 85, 87, 88,
    89, 91, 92, 93, 96, 97, 102, 103, 112,
    115, 118, 124
time frame, 31
time series, 93
tracking, 126
tradition, 85
training, 9, 18, 19, 66, 77, 115, 120
transition, 10, 24, 110
transport, 73
transportation, 6, 12, 18, 36, 67, 70, 107,
    113
tribes, 10, 12, 13
trust, 59, 107
turnover, 62, 101
tutoring, 6

U

unemployment, 3, 97, 111
United States, 1, 5, 24
universities, 83

V

Valencia, 131
variation, 14, 61, 66, 67
victims, 12, 13
Vietnam, 116
village, 15
violence, 12, 61
vision, 66, 90, 92
voice, 67
voice mail, 67
voters, 108
vouchers, 15, 20, 78, 119

W

wages, 115
warrants, 72, 82
welfare, 2, 10, 46, 69, 77, 118, 126
well-being, 11
White House, 3
winter, 69
women, 4, 18, 58, 77, 97, 102
work, 19, 22, 23, 38, 39, 41, 43, 44, 47,
    51, 52, 54, 58, 61, 64, 65, 70, 72, 77,
    78, 79, 82, 87, 88, 91, 113, 115, 120
workers, 48, 51, 55, 56, 61, 65, 72, 75,
    76, 79, 94, 103, 120
worry, 119
writing, 34, 38